T063316?

Edible Seattle: The Cookbook

EDIBLE SEATTLE: THE COOKBOOK

EDITED BY JILL LIGHTNER

PHOTOGRAPHS BY CAROLE TOPALIAN

STERLING EPICURE
New York

STERLING EPICURE
New York

An Imprint of Sterling Publishing
387 Park Avenue South
New York, NY 10016

STERLING EPICURE is a trademark of Sterling Publishing Co., Inc.
The distinctive Sterling logo is a registered trademark of Sterling Publishing Co., Inc.

Text and photographs © 2012 by Edible Communities, Inc.

All rights reserved. No part of this publication may be reproduced, stored in a retrieval system,
or transmitted, in any form or by any means, electronic, mechanical, photocopying, recording,
or otherwise, without prior written permission from the publisher.

ISBN 978-1-4027-8555-9 (hardcover)
ISBN 978-1-4027-9834-4 (ebook)

Library of Congress Cataloging-in-Publication Data

Edible Seattle : the cookbook / edited by Jill Lightner ; photographs by Carole Topalian.
    p. cm.
Includes index.
ISBN 978-1-4027-8555-9
 1. Cooking—Washington (State) 2. Cooking—Washington (State)—Seattle. 3. Local foods—Washington (State)
4. Cooking, American—Pacific Northwest style. 5. Cookbooks. I. Lightner, Jill.
TX715.2.P32E35 2012
641.59797'772—dc23
2011033770

Distributed in Canada by Sterling Publishing
c/o Canadian Manda Group, 165 Dufferin Street
Toronto, Ontario, Canada M6K 3H6
Distributed in the United Kingdom by GMC Distribution Services
Castle Place, 166 High Street, Lewes, East Sussex, England BN7 1XU
Distributed in Australia by Capricorn Link (Australia) Pty. Ltd.
P.O. Box 704, Windsor, NSW 2756, Australia

For information about custom editions, special sales, and premium and corporate purchases,
please contact Sterling Special Sales at 800-805-5489 or specialsales@sterlingpublishing.com.

Manufactured in the United States of America

2 4 6 8 10 9 7 5 3 1

www.sterlingpublishing.com

Contents

FOREWORD

What you hold in your hand is the second in a new generation of community cookbooks.

It's thoroughly cutting edge—gleaned from the kitchens and pantries of the chefs, bakers, experimental food bloggers, mushroom hunters, herb gardeners, and avid eaters that have built Seattle's food community. But *Edible Seattle: The Cookbook* is also an old soul—kin to the community cookbooks that have been published by churches, schools and other collections of like-minded individuals throughout North America for centuries.

Communities crave cookbooks. In fact, they need them. They need them to document and codify food traditions; to remind us of what's in season; to chronicle and celebrate the people in our communities who feed and sustain us. No matter if today's cookbook is organized by urban CSA members or the teachers behind an edible schoolyard project. Or if recipes once gathered on ruled cards are now crowd-sourced on email. The mission remains the same.

This same mission was part of the inspiration for *Edible Ojai*, the first Edible magazine, launched in 2002. The simple and revolutionary idea—which has now manifested in nearly 70 Edible magazines in big cities, little towns and everywhere in between— was that telling the story behind our food would encourage us all to eat better, restore our landscape, support our neighbors and generally make food and drink experiences a bigger, richer part of our collective lives.

In a project that began with Brooklyn, and continues with Seattle, Dallas-Fort Worth, the Twin Cities, and an extensive list of distinct culinary regions throughout the United States and Canada, Edible Communities will publish a series of cookbooks that celebrate those areas where Edible magazines exist. In keeping with the pages of local Edible magazines, these cookbooks invite 100 or so people from the food community to submit original recipes that tell something about their place and their place in it.

This particular installation celebrates the splendid regional ingredients of Western Washington. You'll find simple dishes like a crisp Romano bean salad with Rhonda Gothberg's feta cheese and a quick bread made with Sherman Farms Sugar Hubbard squash alongside the more exotic flavors of chana masala made with Yakima chickpeas and Pike Place Market spices. We hope you'll experiment with Jerry Traunfeld's sea bean fritters, go foraging for the Herbfarm's Douglas fir syrup and taste the utter decadence of Heather Earnhardt's salted caramel chocolate tart.

Wherever you may be, please consider this cookbook inspiration to get to know the people who feed you.

—Tracey Ryder, Cofounder, Edible Communities, Inc.; Alex Corcoran, Publisher, *Edible Seattle*

COLUMBIA CITY FARMERS MARKET

INTRODUCTION

Seattle is the biggest small town in the country. Not only does every citizen have multiple connections to everyone else, but we all love to talk about each other, preferably over coffee and snacks. We nibble and gossip and tell lengthy stories about how our neighbor was one of Bill Gates Jr.'s high school teachers. We run into one of our world-class chefs at the farmers' market and chat about their kid's science fair project, not their recent restaurant award. When we drop names, it's not a celebrity thing—it's a "let me introduce you, y'all would hit it off" thing.

We're also a city of nerds. Remember that survey that netted us "smartest U.S. city" status? The simple fact that we're collectively a bunch of smarty-pants shows up everywhere you look. A bunch of our farmers and food artisans are retired engineers, software designers, and medical professionals, which is why visiting a farmers' market here is such an education. We've got farmers on the cutting edge of biodiesel and wind power, chemical engineers crafting cider and sharing fermentation technology, nurses tending goats and making cheese, and tech workers who spend their off-hours foraging in the mountains. We love sharing information with each other, and there's a strong collective belief that education is always a net positive. Ask an orchardist about an apple and you'll get an answer that combines 200 years of history with a dose of agricultural policy politics and as much insight into organic growing methods as you care to listen to. You'll also be handed a slice to taste, of course—think of it as the spoonful of sugar helping the medicine go down.

When we set out to collect the recipes for this book, we tried to think specifically about what makes Seattle such a fun place to eat. There's the prevalence of the seasonal menu, for sure, which has made unpopular vegetables like kale and parsnips into superstars here. There's our sweet tooth—pie and cupcakes aren't trends in Seattle; they're permanent fixtures of our diet. There's our dedication to gardening, for both chefs and nonprofessional cooks. Bees, chickens, and canning are part of that package, as is a willingness to help nurture heirloom varieties by planting them in our raised beds. There's wild seafood, of course, and wild mushrooms. There's the delicious reality that, with our rich soil and the varied climates throughout the state, Washington can produce any food that's not straight-up tropical. Heck, we've even got a citrus that grows nicely in the Cascade foothills. There's the strong presence of Southeast Asia and North Africa among our citizenry, particularly in the Rainier Valley. And, maybe most important, there's the fact that we're a bunch of sociable small-town-in-a-big-city folks who love to get together over food, both in and out of our homes.

While plenty of these recipes come from local chefs, we steered clear of anything too complex—we want these recipes to get used, rather than just admired in theory. We might nudge you out of your comfort zone a bit, toward rabbit or seaweed or *za'atar* or duck eggs, but we're guessing you're up for a bit of adventure, as long as you can sit back with a big slice of fresh peach pie afterward and tell all your friends the tale of how you foraged for seaweed—and what you learned about marine biology, Japanese culture, and soup making in the process.

—Jill Lightner, *Edible Seattle*

TAYLOR SHELLFISH FARM, SAMISH BAY

CHAPTER 1

STARTERS

Seattle's famously unpredictable weather patterns make for some odd dining habits; there's been more than one Fourth of July that required mittens, and more than one Valentine's Day when dinner could have been served al fresco. With that in mind, we selected our starters to reflect the need for warm grilled salads to enjoy on those frustratingly cold summer nights, and even a few cold dishes that make optimum use of winter's finest ingredients.

Simple appetizers are also a low-pressure way to play around with unusual ingredients. Glasswort? Seaweed? Emmer? Pickled rhubarb? Not all at once (no need to panic), but we think people are more likely to try these locally sourced ingredients—and be pleasantly surprised—if there's the reassurance of a more familiar meal to follow.

RHUBARB BRUSCHETTA

From Lara Ferroni

In 2010, we set out to prove that rhubarb—that inescapable sign that spring has arrived in Seattle gardens—is for more than just sweet dishes. In fact, before our sweet-toothed pioneers came to call it "pie plant," rhubarb was considered more of a medicinal remedy than anything else.

Lara's springtime bruschetta is spicy, herbal, tangy, crisp, and just about everything delicious except sweet. The topping is a little like a pico de gallo, with rhubarb taking the place of tomatoes. Its cheerful colors are about the prettiest thing you could possibly eat on a cloudy spring day. In a nod to modern fusion cuisine, the pickled rhubarb is also lovely on top of *carnitas*—blending a traditional English springtime dish with your favorite taco truck. It might raise some eyebrows if you serve it on Cinco de Mayo, but it'll be far tastier than an out-of-season tomato.

2 STALKS RHUBARB, DICED
2 TBSP MINCED RED ONION
½ TSP SEA SALT
½ TSP FRESH THYME LEAVES
1 TBSP SHERRY VINEGAR
⅛ TSP DRY MUSTARD
2 TBSP EXTRA-VIRGIN OLIVE OIL,
   PLUS MORE FOR BRUSHING
   THE TOAST

12 SLICES BAGUETTE
MICROGREENS FOR GARNISH

Makes 12 slices of toast
Vegan

1 Preheat the broiler or grill. Mix the rhubarb, onion, and sea salt in a small bowl and let sit for 2 minutes. Stir in the thyme, vinegar, mustard, and olive oil. Let stand for at least another 10 minutes.

2 Brush each slice of baguette on both sides with olive oil, and grill or broil until the edges just turn dark brown. Leave in the warm (but turned-off) oven until the toast is crisp all the way through.

3 To serve, top each slice of toast with a heaping spoon of the rhubarb mixture and add a few microgreens for garnish.

Edible Tip

Don't place the topping on the toast until you're ready to eat—otherwise, the bread will get soggy. For a picnic or potluck, carry the topping separate from the toast and put the bruschetta together on-site. It's fine if the toast is at room temperature.

APPLE CRAB CAKES WITH PICKLED APPLE-FENNEL SLAW

From Jess Thomson

Crab cake preferences are divided by coast, but wherever you're from, we think you'll agree that a good crab cake is about the crab, not the filler. Jess's bite-size cakes are packed with crab, just held together with panko crumbs, and nicely accessorized with apple. Because these can be fried in advance and reheated, they make a terrific party snack. We think an apple in the midrange between tart and sweet works best here, accentuating the natural sweetness of the Dungeness. Look for Jonagold, Elstar, or King of Tompkins County (sometimes just labeled King) on farmers' market tables in the fall. And while you're poking around those tables, look for locally made apple cider vinegar for the slaw. When cider vinegar is done right, a pure apple flavor shines through the acidity, and your final slaw will be a different creature than if you use a mass-produced product.

Edible Cider Pairing

Red Barn Cider's Jonagold semidry cider—using Skagit Valley Jonagold apples—has plenty of rich apple flavor and bright acidity. Its balanced sweetness is terrific with the naturally sweet crab meat, and the perfect counterpart to the tangy slaw.

FOR THE SLAW:
½ BULB FENNEL, THINLY SLICED, THEN SLICED AGAIN INTO SHORT BATONS
1 LARGE APPLE, THINLY SLICED, THEN SLICED AGAIN INTO SHORT BATONS
1 TBSP CHOPPED FRESH PARSLEY
3 TBSP APPLE CIDER VINEGAR

FOR THE CRAB CAKES:
1 TBSP EXTRA-VIRGIN OLIVE OIL
¾ CUP FINELY CHOPPED ONION
1 CUP FINELY CHOPPED LEEK (WHITE AND GREEN PARTS)
SALT
FRESHLY GROUND BLACK PEPPER
1 MEDIUM APPLE, PEELED, CORED, AND DICED
4 SCALLIONS, WHITE AND GREEN PARTS, CHOPPED
2 LARGE EGGS, BEATEN
1 CUP PANKO BREADCRUMBS
1 LB DUNGENESS CRAB MEAT, CHOPPED
1 TBSP CHOPPED FRESH PARSLEY
VEGETABLE OIL FOR FRYING

Serves 8–10
Dairy-free

Make the slaw:

1 Blend the fennel, apple, and parsley together in a small bowl. Toss with the vinegar. Cover the bowl and set aside at room temperature.

Make the crab cakes:

2 Heat a medium skillet over medium heat. Add the olive oil, then the onion and leek. Season to taste with salt and pepper, and cook, stirring, until soft, about 5 minutes. Stir in the apple and scallions and remove from the heat.

3 In a large bowl, stir the eggs, breadcrumbs, and crab together with a large fork until blended. Season to taste with salt and pepper. Add the apple mixture and parsley and stir to mix well.

4 Heat a large, heavy skillet over medium-high heat. Add enough vegetable oil to fill the pan about ½ inch deep. When a small piece of crab sizzles vigorously in the pan, add the crab by packed tablespoons to the hot oil, taking care not to crowd the pan. Cook about 2 minutes undisturbed, until browned. Flip the crab cakes carefully and cook another 2 minutes. Drain the cooked cakes on a paper towel–lined plate and repeat with the remaining crab mixture, adjusting the oil temperature as necessary.

5 Serve the crab cakes hot, each topped with a dollop of the slaw.

CHANTERELLE PUFFS

An appetizing combination of toasted cheese and buttery wild mushrooms, these puffs are the sort of treat that impresses guests without truly requiring much effort. Any meaty mushroom (even the standard button variety) will work nicely if chanterelles are either out of season or out of your price range.

If you're truly crazy about chanterelles, it might be time to check out a class from the Puget Sound Mycological Society (see Resources, page 162). These well-trained folks provide classes on beginning and intermediate mushroom identification, as well as member field trips. Since Western Washington is, during most years, overflowing with mushrooms (and chanterelles are a great one for beginners), these classes can easily pay for themselves in a single season. More important, they provide a great excuse for wandering around in a nearby forest.

Edible Tip

Golden Glen Creamery in Bow makes a terrific Parmesan that is lovely in these puffs (see Resources, page 162).

1 TBSP EXTRA-VIRGIN OLIVE OIL
1 CUP MINCED CHANTERELLES (OR A MIX OF WILD MUSHROOM VARIETIES)
½ STICK (4 TBSP) UNSALTED BUTTER
¼ TSP SALT
⅓ CUP ALL-PURPOSE FLOUR
3 LARGE EGGS
1 CUP FINELY GRATED PARMESAN CHEESE

Makes about 35 puffs
Vegetarian

1 Heat the olive oil in a small saucepan over medium-high heat. When hot, add the chanterelles and sauté for about 4 minutes, until heated through and slightly tender. Remove from the heat.

2 Preheat the oven to 425°F. Lightly grease 2 baking sheets, preferably the noninsulated kind.

3 In a heavy medium saucepan over medium-high heat, combine the butter, 1 cup water, and the salt. Bring the mixture to a boil, stirring constantly, until the butter is completely melted. Adjust the heat to medium and add the flour all at once. Continue cooking, stirring constantly, until the mixture starts to form a ball, about 5 minutes. The dough should be smooth and fairly stiff. Remove the saucepan from the heat.

4 Add the eggs to the dough, one at a time, and mix thoroughly after each addition. When the eggs are fully incorporated and the batter is glossy, stir in the cheese and sautéed chanterelles and mix well to combine.

5 Drop heaping teaspoons of batter onto the prepared baking sheets, leaving about an inch between heaps of batter. Bake until puffed up and golden brown, 13–15 minutes. Serve warm.

EMMER FRIES

From Ashley Rodriguez

While Ashley's emmer fries aren't quite the same as the locally famous ones served at Emmer & Rye, the inspiration came from the same place: Brooke and Sam Lucy of Bluebird Grain Farms. Bluebird was one of the earliest growers of emmer in the state, and its emmer can be found in restaurants all over town, particularly in far-rottos (like risotto, but made with emmer, whose Italian name is farro). These fries are based on cracked emmer, a minimally processed ancient grain that's high in protein and has a distinct nutty flavor.

4 CUPS WHOLE MILK
1 CUP WATER
2 TBSP UNSALTED BUTTER
2 ¼ CUPS CRACKED EMMER
1 CUP GRATED GRUYÈRE
½ CUP GRATED PARMESAN
½ TSP FRESH THYME LEAVES
SALT

FRESHLY GROUND BLACK PEPPER
½ CUP OLIVE OIL FOR FRYING,
    PLUS MORE AS NEEDED
FLOUR FOR DUSTING

Serves 6–8
Vegetarian

1 Lightly oil a 13 x 9-inch metal baking pan. Bring the milk, water, and butter to a boil in a large, heavy saucepan over high heat. Gradually whisk in the emmer. Reduce the heat to low and cook until tender, about 20 minutes. Remove from the heat and stir in both cheeses and the thyme. Season to taste with salt and pepper.

2 Immediately transfer the emmer to the prepared baking pan, spreading evenly to cover the bottom. Refrigerate until cool and firm, about 1 hour. (The emmer can be prepared up to 1 day ahead. Cover and keep refrigerated.)

3 Cut the chilled emmer lengthwise in the pan into 3 (3-inch-wide) rectangles. Cut each rectangle crosswise into ¾-inch-wide strips. Set the strips aside.

4 Preheat the oven to 300°F. Heat the olive oil in a large, heavy skillet over medium-high heat. Place the flour in a pie plate. Lightly coat the emmer strips with flour; shake off the excess. Working in batches, fry the strips until golden brown on all sides, about 5 minutes, adding more oil as necessary.

5 Using a slotted spoon or tongs, transfer the fries to paper towels to absorb excess oil. Place the fries on a baking sheet and keep warm in the oven while cooking the remaining batches. Transfer the fries to large platter and serve with the dipping sauce of your choice.

CHEESE-STUFFED MUSHROOMS

Washington has more kinds of wild mushrooms than almost anywhere in the world—but sometimes all you really need is a handy edible container, and that's where button mushrooms come in. These are still Washington-grown: Ostrom's is an Olympia-based company with more than 250 employees, and you can find their mushrooms at grocery stores all over the region. For this recipe, you want caps sized so you can fit the whole thing in your mouth at once (unless, of course, you're the sort who secretly enjoys watching friends drop half a mushroom's worth of filling down their front).

20 SMALL TO MEDIUM BUTTON
   MUSHROOMS
1 TBSP EXTRA-VIRGIN OLIVE OIL
2 SHALLOTS, MINCED
3 CLOVES GARLIC, MINCED
⅓ CUP MARSALA
¼ TSP FRESH THYME LEAVES
¼ TSP FRESH ROSEMARY LEAVES,
   MINCED

FRESHLY GROUND BLACK PEPPER
½ CUP LABNEH
½ CUP CRUMBLED CHÈVRE

Makes 20 mushroom caps
Vegetarian
Gluten-free

1 Preheat the oven to 350°F. Line a baking sheet with parchment paper. Pull or cut the stems out of the mushroom caps and gently brush the caps free of any dirt. Reserve the stems for another use or simply compost them.

2 In a medium sauté pan over medium heat, warm the olive oil. Sauté the shallots and garlic until fragrant, 2–3 minutes. Pour in the Marsala and scrape up any browned bits from the bottom of the pan. Let the wine cook down into a thick paste that coats the shallots. Stir in the thyme, rosemary, and pepper to taste. Remove from the heat.

3 In a small bowl, blend together the *labneh* and chèvre. Stir in the shallot-Marsala mixture. Using a ½ teaspoon measure or small demitasse spoon, fill each mushroom cap with enough filling to mound just slightly above the edge of the cap. Place them at least 1 inch apart on the prepared baking sheet and bake until they're hot all the way through and the mushrooms are starting to wrinkle or shrink, about 15 minutes. Let rest for at least 2 minutes before serving.

Edible Tip

Labneh is a seriously thick yogurt cheese—fromage blanc is similar, but less tangy. Samish Bay makes an incredible *labneh* that Jess Thomson once attempted to describe as "like licking a cow. In a good way." We know what she means: there's pure, concentrated dairy bliss in their *labneh*.

If you can't get your hands on *labneh*, you can substitute any number of similarly thick cultured milk products—fromage blanc, quark, or even whole-milk Greek yogurt. The consistency of the filling won't change; just the slight tanginess will vary according to the product.

SEA BEAN TEMPURA

From Jerry Traunfeld,
Poppy Restaurant

In Seattle, it's easier to pick your own sea beans than it is to find them in stores or at markets, although sometimes the Foraged & Found table will have them available at farmers' markets. Sea beans, also known as glasswort or salicornia, can be harvested on the Olympic Peninsula or around Puget Sound—they're grassy succulents that thrive on beaches throughout the world. Not at all bean-like, sea beans are skinny little straws of succulent crispness. They naturally contain a fair amount of salt (so would you if you spent your life photosynthesizing on the edge of the ocean), so it's important to hide your saltcellar before cooking this, lest you automatically sprinkle some on the fritters after frying.

Edible Tip

Surprisingly, harvesting sea beans doesn't require a foraging permit. You should still check for water-quality issues ahead of time; it's not known for certain whether bacteria in the water will affect the nearby plants. You should also make sure that any beach you'd like to pick allows harvesting; for instance, it's illegal to gather any type of plant from national and state parks.

1 QT VEGETABLE OIL FOR DEEP
  FRYING
1 CUP ALL-PURPOSE FLOUR
1 TBSP CORNSTARCH
1 TSP BAKING POWDER
1¼–1½ CUPS ICE WATER

¼ LB SEA BEANS
ACCOMPANIMENT: SOY- OR
  DASHI-BASED DIPPING SAUCE

Makes about 16 pieces
Vegan

1 In a medium-size saucepan, heat the oil to 375°F (check the temperature using a deep-fry or candy thermometer).

2 Stir the flour, cornstarch, and baking powder together in a medium-size bowl. Using chopsticks, stir in enough of the ice water to make a lumpy batter, with the consistency of light cream.

3 Drop a small bundle of sea beans into the batter and coat thoroughly. Gather them with your fingers and drop the bunch into the hot oil. Repeat the procedure with several more bunches, taking care not to crowd them in the saucepan. Fry until lightly browned and crisp. Drain on paper towels, and repeat with the remaining sea beans.

4 Serve hot with a soy- or dashi-based dipping sauce.

GREEK NACHOS

A few years back, a friend had a ridiculous—but highly compelling—restaurant idea, summarized in the name International House of Nachos. Truth is, once you start thinking on the basic idea of a crunchy chip, topped with a spiced protein and a gooey cheese, it's easy to come up with delicious variations. This is one that stuck around well after we stopped laughing about a globe-trotting nacho-themed menu. It uses Whidbey Island heirloom Rockwell beans, which cook quickly after an overnight soak. You could also use Stoney Plains cannellini beans.

The fresh herbs are important here, so this is best served as a summer or fall dish, when you can pick everything from your own garden. Celery leaves have great flavor—like celery, only more so. When you want the flavor but not the texture of celery, they're a fresh-tasting alternative to celery seeds.

FOR THE TZATZIKI:
1 CUP WHOLE-MILK GREEK YOGURT
1 CUP GRATED CUCUMBER
1 CLOVE GARLIC, MINCED
1 TSP MINCED FRESH DILL
¼ TSP SALT

FOR THE NACHOS:
1½ CUPS DRIED ROCKWELL BEANS
1 FRESH BAY LEAF
½–¾ TSP KOSHER SALT
5 TBSP EXTRA-VIRGIN OLIVE OIL
2 TBSP MINCED CELERY LEAVES

½ TSP MINCED FRESH GREEK
   OREGANO
½ TSP FRESH THYME LEAVES
1 TSP FRESH LEMON JUICE
FRESHLY GROUND BLACK PEPPER
8 PIECES PITA BREAD
¼ CUP SLIVERED KALAMATA
   OLIVES, OR MORE TO TASTE
1 CUP GRATED MYZITHRA CHEESE
ZA'ATAR TO TASTE

Serves 4
Vegetarian

Make the tzatziki:

1 Combine the yogurt, cucumber, garlic, dill, and salt in a medium bowl. This can be made up to 48 hours in advance; store covered in the refrigerator.

Make the nachos:

2 In a large bowl, soak the beans in 2 quarts of water overnight. The next day, drain and rinse the beans. In a medium saucepan, combine them with the bay leaf and 1 quart of cold water. Simmer the beans over medium heat, stirring occasionally and adding more water as needed, until they are soft and creamy, 70–90 minutes. Salt them generously—between ½ and ¾ teaspoon, total—in the pot with any remaining water and let sit for 5 minutes. Drain any remaining water from the beans and remove the bay leaf.

3 Pour the beans into a large bowl and drizzle with 3 tablespoons of the olive oil. Sprinkle with the celery leaves, oregano, and thyme. Mash everything together with a potato masher, until the mixture is midway between smooth and chunky. Blend in the lemon juice and season to taste with pepper. If the dip is thicker than you'd like, thin it out with a little water. Set the bean dip aside on the counter.

Za'atar is a Middle Eastern condiment spice blend that blends sumac, sesame seeds, and thyme, with regional variations abounding. We love it with all Mediterranean or Fertile Crescent dishes (and use it for Shakshouka, page 116). World Spice sells two versions: Israeli and Syrian. For this dish, opt for the Israeli version.

4 Preheat the oven to 400°F. Pour the remaining 2 tablespoons olive oil into a small bowl. Brush each pita lightly with the oil, sprinkle with salt, and cut each into 8–10 wedges. Arrange the wedges in a single layer on a half sheet pan. Bake until the wedges are light brown and getting crispy, about 4 minutes. Remove the pan from the oven, but leave the heat on.

5 Stir the pita chips around in the pan, so some are in layers and others are still in a single layer. Drop generous dollops of the bean dip on top of the chips. Dot with slivers of the olives to your liking and sprinkle generously with the *myzithra* cheese. Bake until the pita wedges are brown and crisp and the cheese is warm, about another 4 minutes. Sprinkle with *za'atar* to taste.

6 To serve, it's easiest for people to help themselves out of the hot pan. Use the tzatziki for dipping.

CAVOLFIORE ARROSTITO

From Brian Gojdics, Tutta Bella

This warm antipasto was a standard for a couple of years at Tutta Bella, and we hope it'll now be a standard in your own kitchen. While the restaurant always made it with white cauliflower, Brian thinks it would be equally great—and downright festive—if made with Romanesco or one of the pretty orange or purple varieties. (If you try a different variety, keep your eye on the broiling time; it's a little trickier to tell when the caramelization is occurring.) Don't let the intense caper-and-anchovy dressing scare you. Once it's mixed in with the warm vegetables, breadcrumbs, and cheese, the flavors fade into the background so you'll be struck not by the anchovy, but by the indecipherably tasty cauliflower. Cauliflower is widely available on our farmers' market tables from April to December, but the interesting varieties and most abundant crops come in from July to September.

FOR THE BREADCRUMBS:
3 CUPS DAY-OLD BREAD CUT INTO A ½-INCH DICE (CIABATTA IS IDEAL)
1 TBSP GRATED PARMIGIANO-REGGIANO CHEESE
1 TSP SEA SALT
SCANT PINCH OF RED PEPPER FLAKES
3 TBSP EXTRA-VIRGIN OLIVE OIL

FOR THE CAULIFLOWER:
1 OIL- OR SALT-PACKED ANCHOVY FILLET
JUICE OF 1 LEMON

1 TBSP CAPERS, DRAINED AND RINSED
1 TBSP PLUS 1 TSP EXTRA-VIRGIN OLIVE OIL
1 HEAD CAULIFLOWER (ABOUT 1 LB)
1 TSP SEA SALT, PLUS MORE TO TASTE
SCANT PINCH OF RED PEPPER FLAKES
3 OZ PARMIGIANO-REGGIANO CHEESE, SHAVED USING A VEGETABLE PEELER

Serves 4

Make the breadcrumbs:

1 Preheat the oven to 300°F. Combine the bread, Parmigiano, salt, and red pepper in a medium bowl and mix well. Drizzle half the olive oil over the bread and toss well. Add the rest of the oil and toss again to make sure there is a nice even coating.

2 Place the bread mixture on a baking sheet in a single layer, being careful not to crowd the pan. Bake until the bread has dried and is browned and crunchy, 45–60 minutes. Let cool, then crush the bread

Edible Tip

This recipe can be made ahead up through the roasting of the cauliflower. Reheat in a 500°F oven and continue with the recipe.

into small pieces (about the size of a BB) in a food processor or by placing them in a zip-top bag and crushing with a rolling pin. Do not crush into a powder; you want a pellet size for texture.

Make the cauliflower:

3 Reset the oven to broil. If your broiler has a choice of temperature settings, set it to high. In a large bowl, mash the anchovy into a paste, using the back of a spoon. Add the lemon juice, capers, and 1 teaspoon of the olive oil and mix together thoroughly. Set aside.

4 Core the cauliflower and break the head down into about 1-inch florets. If the core has any tough skin on the outside, peel it and cut it into ½-inch pieces. Toss the cauliflower with the remaining 1 tablespoon olive oil and the sea salt. Place in a 9 x 13-inch baking pan and place underneath the hot broiler. Broil, stirring occasionally, until the cauliflower is lightly caramelized and just cooked through—preferably a touch toothy. This will take 6–10 minutes. Be careful to not overcook the cauliflower because it will turn to mush.

5 While the roasted cauliflower is still hot, toss it in a large bowl with the anchovy dressing. As the cauliflower begins to cool, it will start to absorb the dressing. Crush half of the Parmigiano shavings and toss them with the cauliflower.

6 To serve, transfer the cauliflower to a platter, top with the remaining shavings of Parmigiano, and sprinkle with the breadcrumbs.

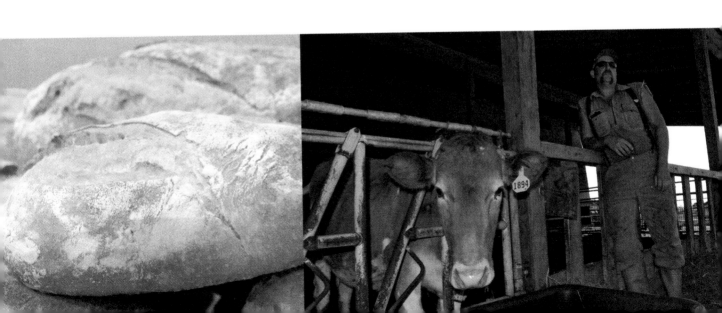

CHARRED ENDIVE WITH FENNEL, BEECHER'S FLAGSHIP CHEDDAR, AND GOLDEN RAISINS

From Bastille Café & Bar

Depending on when hot weather kicks in during our unpredictable summers, fat, crisp fennel bulbs can show up in early August and stick around through fall. While fennel is often described as tasting like licorice, that's a bit like declaring that a button mushroom tastes like a morel. Fresh fennel is fragrant with a whisper of grassy anise-licorice flavor, but the eating experience is really more about its crisp, light texture and musky sweetness. It's a lovely counterpoint to the very slightly bitter endive.

Served before just about any grilled meal, from burgers, steak, and lamb kebabs to chicken and salmon, this salad will spark up your taste buds. With a frosty pitcher of chamomile cordial or lemonade made with Elderflower Syrup (page 159), you'll be able to cool off and enjoy a warm summer evening in perfect comfort.

½ CUP DRY WHITE WINE
¼ CUP GOLDEN RAISINS
1 FENNEL BULB WITH TOP
½ TSP CRACKED ANISE SEEDS
SEA SALT
⅔ CUP PLUS 1 TBSP EXTRA-VIRGIN OLIVE OIL

4 BELGIUM ENDIVES
6 OZ BEECHER'S FLAGSHIP CHEDDAR, CRUMBLED
COARSE SEA SALT

Serves 4

1 Combine the wine and raisins in a small saucepan and bring to a simmer over medium heat. Simmer until the raisins are plump, about 5 minutes. Remove from the heat.

2 Remove the top from the fennel, reserving the fronds. Remove the outer layer of the fennel bulb and discard. Using a mandoline or handheld slicer, shave the fennel bulb and the branch as thin as possible across the grain. In a medium bowl, combine the shaved fennel, anise seeds, fennel fronds, salt, and ⅔ cup of the olive oil to create a dressing. Set aside at room temperature.

3 Preheat a gas grill to 400°F or warm a large cast-iron skillet over high heat. Peel away the outer layers of the endives and quarter the heads, leaving the root on to hold the quarters together. Gently toss the quartered endives with the remaining 1 tablespoon olive oil and sea salt to taste. Place the endives on the grill and char about 4 minutes on each side. (Be patient: moving the endive too much will cause it to fall apart and become soggy.)

4 Gently toss together the warm endives, raisins, and fennel dressing. Divide among 4 salad plates and sprinkle with the crumbled cheddar. Garnish with coarse sea salt to taste.

Edible Tip

If you can't get your hands on Beecher's Flagship cheddar, we suggest either Rhonda Gothberg's goat cheddar or Golden Glen Creamery's sharp cheddar or their double cream River cheddar. A good nonlocal choice is Kerrygold—the goal is a sharp, tangy flavor.

JAMES HALL

Taylor Shellfish

Taylor Shellfish farmers are all essentially scientists, regardless of what they farm. The science that James Hall uses relates to the tides and to marine biology—even though he's neither oceanographer nor marine biologist. James has worked for Taylor Shellfish since 1982, and he farms oysters. More specifically, he's the farm manager behind an entirely new eating experience for oyster lovers. On a 1,000-acre patch of Samish Bay, James oversees one of the two Shigoku beds in existence. Shigoku means "ultimate" in Japanese, and as anyone lucky enough to have eaten a Shigoku will agree, they're as good as an oyster gets. It's not a different species that led to this greatness, but rather a simple technology shift.

The idea for the Shigoku evolved from the British Columbia–grown Kusshi. The technique in both instances begins with a Pacific oyster. Left in their natural state, Pacifics are a perfectly acceptable oyster, but they're nobody's favorite. They're resilient in tough conditions, and the vast majority of our bays qualify as "tough conditions" these days—acidity, pollution, increasingly unpredictable weather patterns, and temperature changes all wreak havoc on an oyster's native habitat. But the Pacific can cope with these difficulties, and a farm in BC had the idea that they could grow the Pacific into something more delicious by mechanically tumbling them in large bags. The movement of the oysters in the bags chips at the shell continually, and as the oyster grows, it develops a thicker, deeper shape. These modified oysters were christened Kusshi oysters and have a meat that is dense and velvety.

Justin Taylor, patriarch of the Taylor Shellfish family, who died in early 2011, thought that his operation could improve upon the Kusshi by letting the ocean do the tumbling instead. The bags are tied to stationary lines that rise and fall with the changes in the tide. The semidiurnal tides (two high and two low tides each day) of Puget Sound provide all the tumbling a growing oyster needs to reach perfection.

The Shigoku takes between 9 and 12 months to reach the perfect size, depending on whether it's grown at Samish Bay or out on the coast at Willapa Bay. A typical shore-based oyster bed takes 3 years to grow an oyster, so the tumbled bag presents a decided improvement on the typical oyster timeline, but otherwise the pros and cons of the shore beds compared to intertidal bags are fairly balanced. On the pro side in favor of the bag: common oyster predators like Dungeness crab and Japanese drills can't munch down on the baby oysters. On the downside, a massive storm was able to wipe out 1,000 bags of Willapa Bay Shigokus right before they were ready for harvest.

When Taylor first offered the Shigokus to the public, chefs promptly went bananas over these thick, sweet oysters. There's a distinct cucumber flavor to their oceany brine, a very clean Pacific Ocean crispness. They're so good that the former belle of the oyster ball, the Kumamoto, is now decidedly less popular in comparison, poor dear. James just laughs when asked how Taylor is doing in its efforts to meet demand. Even with the shorter time to maturity, and assuming that another massive storm doesn't take out Willapa Bay, it's clear it'll be a long while before Taylor catches up.

CUCUMBER SORBET WITH SHIGOKU OYSTERS

Shigoku oysters—the tiny, dense, thick oysters grown by Taylor Shellfish—are tumbled by the tides twice a day, which slowly chips their shells so that the little mollusks grow in tidy little cup shapes. It's a very dainty bite of ocean, and while they're essentially perfect just as they are, we also like to highlight their light cucumber crispness with a tiny dab of cucumber sorbet. Shigokus are still hard to come by—chefs around the country are snapping them up as fast as they're grown—and are at their peak in late winter, around January and February. This means you'll be using nonlocal cucumbers for the sorbet. If you can find them, opt for Persian (grown in central California, typically). They have a dense, flavorful sweetness that's hard to beat. If you want to make the sorbet when local cukes are in season, look for Japanese varieties.

⅓ CUP SUGAR
⅓ CUP WATER
1 OZ GIN
4–7 CUCUMBERS (ENOUGH TO MAKE 3 CUPS PURÉED), DEPENDING ON THE SIZE, PEELED AND SEEDED
FRESH LIME JUICE

1 DOZEN SHIGOKU OYSTERS

Makes 1 quart sorbet, enough to serve with dozens of oysters
Gluten-free
Dairy-free

1 Combine the sugar, water, and gin in a small saucepan over medium heat. Bring just to a boil, stir to completely dissolve the sugar, and remove from the heat. Cool to room temperature.

2 In a food processor or blender, puree the cucumbers until completely smooth. Measure out 3 cups of the puree (any remaining puree can be added to a refreshing gin and tonic), stir it into the ginned-up simple syrup, and add fresh lime juice to taste.

3 Chill the mixture for several hours, until it's completely cold. Freeze according to your ice cream maker's manufacturer instructions. Pour the fresh sorbet into a plastic tub and freeze for at least another hour.

4 When you're ready to eat the oysters, shuck them and lay them on the half shell in a pie plate or serving dish filled with crushed ice. Put a few scoops of sorbet in a small bowl and place it in the center of the icy serving dish. Right before people eat their oysters, have them place a small dab of the sorbet on top. The leftover sorbet is delicious on its own, or toss a scoop into a tall glass of seltzer or Dry cucumber soda for a refreshing cooler.

Edible Wine Pairing

2009 CMS WHITE FROM HEDGES FAMILY ESTATE IN THE COLUMBIA VALLEY, $13

This blend, featuring primarily the Sauvignon Blanc grape, has a racy acidity and bright citrus flavor that make it a natural partner for Shigoku oysters.

WARM ASPARAGUS SALAD
WITH CREAMY TARRAGON VINAIGRETTE

From Jess Thomson

Once we have a few sunny afternoons in a row, Seattle as a whole decides that life is best lived outdoors, and we end up freezing our collective butt off in an al fresco dining attempt in mid-April. You know those dinners—where you end up first turning on the porch or deck lights earlier than you planned, then finding sweaters, and finally giving up and moving inside so your guests stop shivering. Yup, it's asparagus season.

Think of this crisp, warm salad as a way of bringing spring inside—where it belongs. Whether you use slim or fat stalks is a matter of personal preference. As long as you trim the ends properly and set the cooking time to correspond to the diameter, your asparagus will be delicious every time.

Edible Tip

The best way to trim asparagus is to snap each stalk by hand, rather than cut them with a knife. Fresh asparagus will snap cleanly at the point where the stalks get tough. You might end up composting more than feels thrifty, but this method ensures that you won't have any stringy bits in your otherwise perfect salad.

1 LB ASPARAGUS, ENDS TRIMMED
2 TSP DIJON MUSTARD
2 TBSP CHAMPAGNE VINEGAR
SALT
FRESHLY GROUND BLACK PEPPER
⅓ CUP EXTRA-VIRGIN OLIVE OIL

1 TBSP FINELY CHOPPED
   FRESH TARRAGON
1 TBSP HEAVY CREAM

Serves 4
Vegetarian
Gluten-free

1 Bring an inch of water to a strong simmer in a large, wide pan. Add the asparagus and cook until crisp-tender, 3–5 minutes, turning a few times. Drain and arrange on a serving platter.

2 Whisk the mustard and vinegar together in a small bowl, along with a bit of salt and pepper. Add the olive oil in a slow, steady stream, whisking until it's completely incorporated. Add the tarragon and cream and whisk again to combine. Season to taste, and then toss the asparagus with the vinaigrette. Serve warm or at room temperature.

PEAR AND PINE NUT SALAD

From Holly Smith, Café Juanita

Pears are too often lumped together with apples—some of the skins are similar, and they're found in the same season, but a ripe pear is more like a peach than an apple. Soft but not mushy, overwhelmingly succulent, floral, creamy—this is what a pear is meant to be. If you described an apple in a similar manner, folks would assume you couldn't tell an apple from your elbow. Holly suggests D'Anjou for this salad, a beautiful, but limiting, choice. Booth Canyon and Rockridge Orchards grow a variety of more obscure pears that offer more complexity. For a pure hit of that creamy succulence, look for Taylor Gold. Or, for a more floral contrast, find White Doyenne, a cream-colored pear that dates back several centuries. Holly specifically requests using real Parmigiano-Reggiano for this, and we agree—primarily because its nearly crumbling texture provides the perfect delicate counterpart to the pears and pine nuts.

2 LARGE RIPE D'ANJOU PEARS
⅓–½ CUP PINE NUTS
1–2 TSP CHOPPED FRESH THYME
2 OZ PARMIGIANO-REGGIANO
CHEESE, PEELED WITH A
VEGETABLE PEELER, PLUS
ADDITIONAL SHAVINGS
FOR GARNISH

ABOUT ¼ CUP WHITE TRUFFLE OIL
JUICE OF ½–1 LEMON
KOSHER SALT

Serves 4
Vegetarian
Gluten-free

1 Slice the pears ⅛ inch thick and gently combine in a medium bowl with the pine nuts, thyme, and Parmigiano. Dress the mixture with the truffle oil, lemon juice, and salt to taste. Taste and adjust the seasoning if necessary, with salt to boost the overall flavor or lemon for acidity.

2 Divide the mixture among 4 chilled salad plates, garnish with fresh curls of Parmigiano, and, if you're feeling extravagant, drizzle with a little more truffle oil.

Edible Tips

For white truffle oil, be sure to seek out the good stuff at La Buona Tavola in Pike Place Market (see Resources, page 162). These days, there are a lot of cheap truffle oils on the market, concocted with artificial adulterants, rather than a slice of the expensive white truffle. Better to go without than to substitute.

These juicy pears all offer slightly different flavor profiles and textures (look for them on market tables and Central Washington fruit stands from late August through December): Abate Fetel, Bosc, Comice, Comtesse Clara Frijs, Conference, Flemish Beauty, Harrow Delight, Red Clapp, and Seckel.

BABY ARUGULA DUNGENESS CRAB SALAD

*From Chester Gerl,
Matt's in the Market*

It's a happy coincidence for the West Coast that citrus and Dungeness crab are both at their sweetest in the middle of winter. This salad is something of a California transplant, with its orange slices and avocado chunks, but thanks to the flakes of our sweet and tender crustacean, it ends up feeling almost like a native. With Washington's Dungeness catch second only to Oregon's, it's easy to find affordable crab meat during prime season—usually early November through the end of the year.

This salad is fancy enough to kick off a holiday meal, but it also fits right in with winter's rich main dishes. It's best of all, perhaps, as the start to a decadent crab feast with friends—follow this salad with Dungeness mac and cheese and a pile of plain steamed crabs.

FOR THE DRESSING:
1 TSP MINCED SHALLOT
1 TBSP DIJON MUSTARD
½ CUP ORANGE JUICE
SALT
FRESHLY GROUND BLACK PEPPER
½ CUP CANOLA OIL

FOR THE SALAD:
6 OZ BABY ARUGULA

8 OZ LIGHTLY TOASTED MARCONA ALMONDS, ROUGHLY CHOPPED
1 AVOCADO, PEELED, PITTED, AND DICED
24 ORANGE SEGMENTS, SEEDED
6 OZ FRESH DUNGENESS CRAB MEAT

Serves 4
Gluten-free
Dairy-free

Make the dressing:

1 Combine the shallot, mustard, orange juice, and salt and pepper to taste in a small bowl; whisk together until well blended. Slowly stir in the oil. Any extra dressing will keep in the refrigerator for up to 1 month.

Make the salad:

2 In a large bowl, combine the arugula, almonds, avocado, and orange segments. Gently toss with the dressing. Divide the salad evenly among 4 salad plates and top each with 1½ ounces of the crab.

Edible Tip

It's sort of astonishing how easy it is to scorch a pan of nuts, even after years spent trying to get it consistently right. If you're the sort who never fails to respond promptly to your oven's timer, go ahead and pour a single layer of almonds into a sheet pan and pop them in the oven at 350°F. Set the timer for 5 minutes, and give them a stir when the beeper goes off. Repeat once or twice more, until they're a richer toasty brown and send out waves of delectable smells. Less careful cooks will fare better with a nonstick skillet on the stove top. Keep the heat to medium and stir gently—don't walk away—for 5–10 minutes, just until you notice the color turning to the perfect toasty brown shade.

AUTUMN JEWEL SALAD

From Abra Bennett

This is a lovely way to take full advantage of that brief, shining moment at the end of November when ripe persimmons are available. They're easiest to find—and cheapest—at Asian groceries or fruit stands (Viet Wah and MacPherson's are both good bets), and you want to make absolutely sure they're perfectly ripe before eating, or the tannins will pucker your mouth so severely you might fear the sensation is permanent. They're fairly easy to grow in Seattle gardens, although the birds will be after them with even more dedication than they show for cherries in June. If you need to pick them before they're fully ripe, you can quickly ripen Fuyu persimmons by tucking them into a paper bag with an apple for a day or two. Their color will turn a slightly deeper orange and they'll become fairly soft, like a perfect peach.

Edible Tip

Verjuice is a highly acidic juice from unripe grapes. Klipsun Vineyards in Washington's Red Mountain AVA makes verjuice, or you can find imported brands at most gourmet grocers.

FOR THE DRESSING:
6 TBSP WALNUT OIL
3 TBSP POMEGRANATE MOLASSES
2 TBSP WHITE VERJUICE OR FRESH LEMON JUICE

FOR THE SALAD:
2 CUPS ARUGULA
1 CUP RADICCHIO
2 CUPS MIXED GREENS

2 FUYU PERSIMMONS, SLICED
2 CUPS HALVED RED GRAPES
1 CUP POMEGRANATE SEEDS
⅔ CUP TOASTED WHOLE MARCONA OR CALIFORNIA ALMONDS
½ CUP CRUMBLED CHÈVRE

Serves 6
Vegetarian
Gluten-free

Make the dressing:

1 Combine the walnut oil, pomegranate molasses, and white verjuice in a small jar with a tight-fitting lid. Shake to emulsify.

Make the salad:

2 Wash the arugula, radicchio, and greens and dry thoroughly. Divide the mixture among 6 salad plates and top each with persimmon slices, grape halves, a generous sprinkle of the pomegranate seeds, almonds, and chèvre.

3 Drizzle each salad to taste with dressing and serve immediately.

NORTHWEST VEGETARIAN HOT AND SOUR SOUP

From Jess Thomson

Dried local mushrooms, kale, and sweet young carrots from early spring markets make this version of a Chinese classic decidedly northwestern. Feel free to substitute other types of kale or chard for the lacinato kale, and spice lovers should try mustard greens for a sinus-clearing kick—you can find them at the Local Roots market table as well as a number of the Hmong-owned flower stands.

Shortly after we published Jess's recipe in the magazine, we were sent a lovely thank-you note from an entire dinner party. This soup was the star of the table, and the diners were so pleased with its flavor that the hostess popped open her laptop to thank us while everyone was still visiting.

Edible Tip

It's important to use dried mushrooms in this recipe for texture reasons, but it's not absolutely necessary to use porcini. Dried shiitakes or crimini will be almost as good, but using fresh mushrooms would tend toward the slimy in this soup.

6 CUPS VEGETABLE BROTH
1 OZ DRIED PORCINI MUSHROOMS
8 OZ FIRM TOFU (ABOUT ½ PACKAGE)
3 TBSP CORNSTARCH
1 TSP SUGAR
2 TSP DARK SESAME OIL
1 TBSP SOY SAUCE
2 TSP CANOLA OIL
2 CARROTS, CUT INTO ⅛-INCH BY 1-INCH STRIPS, OR SHREDDED IN A FOOD PROCESSOR
3 LEAVES LACINATO (DINOSAUR) KALE, TOUGH RIBS REMOVED AND CUT ACROSS INTO ¼-INCH-WIDE STRIPS

3 TBSP DISTILLED WHITE VINEGAR, OR TO TASTE
½ TSP FRESHLY GROUND WHITE PEPPER, OR TO TASTE
1 LARGE EGG, BEATEN

Serves 4
Vegetarian
Gluten-free (if made with gluten-free soy sauce)
Dairy-free

1 Bring the broth to a boil in a large pot. Add the mushrooms, remove the pot from the heat, and let sit until the mushrooms are soft, about 30 minutes.

2 Meanwhile, cut the tofu into ¼-inch-thick batons; set aside. Blend the cornstarch, 3 tablespoons cold water, and the sugar, sesame oil, and soy sauce together with a fork in a small bowl; set aside.

3 When the mushrooms have softened, remove them from the broth with a slotted spoon and cut into thin strips. (Reserve the broth.)

4 Heat a wok over high heat. When hot, add the canola oil, then the carrots, kale, and mushrooms. Cook, stirring, until the carrots are soft, about 2 minutes. Add the broth (leaving any mushroom grit in the bottom of the pot), then the tofu, and bring to a simmer.

5 Stir the cornstarch mixture, add it to the soup, and bring it back to a simmer, stirring occasionally until the soup looks a bit thicker and almost glossy. Remove the pot from the heat, stir in the vinegar and pepper, and taste for seasoning—you may want a bit more vinegar or pepper. Stir the mixture slowly, creating a gentle whirlpool. Stop stirring, and drizzle the egg in (it will cook upon contact). Serve immediately.

CHESTNUT, APPLE, AND CELERIAC SOUP

From Bobby Moore,
Executive Chef, Barking Frog

If you're mulling over how to start a meal that needs to be as impressive as possible with absolutely minimal effort, look no further. This beautiful fall soup combines two mildly nutty ingredients (celeriac and chestnuts) with tangy apples and apple cider vinegar. At first glance, it sounds far too fancy to make for yourself (who makes pretty garnishes for bowls of soup anyway?), but the actual soup is no more complicated than slicing an apple for a snack—and the garnish comes together in a few minutes while the finished soup stays warm on the back of the stove.

Edible Tip

Frozen chestnuts are most commonly found in Asian grocery stores. Viet Wah, Saar's, Uwajimaya, and H Mart will all have them (see Resources, page 162). In the wintertime, you can find and substitute (more expensive) jarred chestnuts from Whole Foods, Big John's PFI, and DeLaurenti.

FOR THE SOUP:

2 FRESH OR 1 DRIED BAY LEAF
1 TSP BLACK PEPPERCORNS
6–10 FRESH SAGE LEAVES
   (DO NOT SUBSTITUTE DRIED)
1 LB FROZEN PEELED CHESTNUTS,
   THAWED
1 LB CELERIAC, PEELED AND
   COARSELY CHOPPED
1 LB APPLES, PEELED, CORED, AND
   COARSELY CHOPPED
HEAVY CREAM, AS NEEDED
1 CUP HONEY
¼ CUP APPLE CIDER VINEGAR
¼ CUP CHAMPAGNE VINEGAR
SALT
FRESHLY GROUND WHITE PEPPER

FOR THE GARNISH:

2 TBSP UNSALTED BUTTER
½ CUP FINELY DICED CELERIAC
½ CUP PEELED AND FINELY DICED
   APPLES
½ CUP FINELY DICED PEELED
   CHESTNUTS
2–3 TBSP HONEY
3 TBSP BOURBON
SALT

Serves 6
Vegetarian
Gluten-free

Make the soup:

1 Combine the bay leaves, peppercorns, and sage in a small muslin bag or metal tea ball.

2 In a large saucepot, combine the chestnuts, celeriac, and apples. Cover by 1 inch with an equal mixture of water and cream; add the bouquet garni. Heat very slowly over low heat and simmer for 2 hours, stirring occasionally. The soup should become smooth and rich.

3 Stir in the honey and both vinegars. Season to taste with salt and white pepper.

Make the garnish:

4 Melt the butter in a small sauté pan over medium-high heat. Add the celeriac and cook for several minutes. Stir in the apple and cook for 2 more minutes. Add the chestnuts. Once all the ingredients are lightly caramelized, stir in enough honey to stick everything together. Pour in the bourbon, which will evaporate almost immediately. Remove the pan from the heat and season to taste with salt.

5 To serve, divide the soup among 6 bowls. Top each bowl with a small heap of the caramelized garnish.

SOOTHING SEAWEED SOUP

From Sumi Hahn

Sumi Hahn wrote numerous stories for us about her Korean father's food-foraging adventures around our nearby forests and beaches, including one involving seaweed, state permits (or the lack thereof), and wrangling bored children on a chilly day at the beach. While it's easier to simply stop by Uwajimaya for a packet of dried wakame seaweed, we suspect this soup tastes even more delicious when sipped after having braved the shore yourself (after—we insist—you've procured the necessary permit). Prime seaweed-foraging seasons are typically in the late spring or early fall, and it's a wonderful excuse for a lazy walk along the beach. While this soup is typically made with beef—and we like how the delicate beefiness complements the briny seaweed—you can also substitute chopped clams for a soup that tastes more intensely of the sea.

8–15 OZ DRIED WAKAME, ACCORDING TO TASTE
½ LB BONELESS LEAN BEEF, CUT INTO THIN, SHORT STRIPS
1 TSP CHOPPED GARLIC
PINCH OF FRESHLY GROUND BLACK PEPPER
1 TBSP SESAME OIL
2 TBSP SOY SAUCE
1 TSP TOASTED SESAME SEEDS
1 SCALLION, CHOPPED

Serves 4
Dairy-free
Gluten-free (if made with gluten-free soy sauce)

1 Soak the dried wakame in lukewarm water for about 10 minutes. While the seaweed is soaking, sprinkle the beef with the garlic, pepper, sesame oil, and 1 tablespoon of the soy sauce. Mix and set aside for 5 minutes. Drain the wakame and cut into 2-inch pieces.

2 In a medium soup pot over medium-high heat, sauté the seasoned beef until partly cooked, 2–3 minutes depending on the size of the strips. Add the wakame and sauté for another 2 minutes. Adjust the heat to medium-low. Add 6 cups water, the remaining 1 tablespoon soy sauce, and the roasted sesame seeds and simmer for 15 minutes.

3 Ladle the soup into bowls and garnish with the scallion just before serving.

Edible Tips

The right beef to use here is thinly sliced and quite lean, and it's easiest if you start with presliced steak. Stack the thin slices and cut into narrow ribbons. Any good butcher can slice some top round steak for you, or use Skagit River Ranch's "beef stir-fry" cut.

Everyone over the age of fifteen who wants to harvest seaweed needs a permit and should check for acceptable locations and seasonal water-quality issues. All the information, including the purchase of permits, is available online at the Washington Department of Fish and Wildlife website (WDFW.wa.gov).

CHAPTER 2

SIDE DISHES

Being a regular farmers' market shopper

creates two problems. In the cooler months, you're faced with an overload of kale, potatoes, and parsnips, and the limited options can be, well, limiting. In hotter weather, the overabundance becomes intimidating: when faced with fifteen unfamiliar vegetables, most of us just grab the carrots and run. These sides—elegant purees, rustic hashes, and crispy grilled medleys—will inspire you through the winter and help you focus in midsummer. From baby turnips to fresh fava beans, the vegetable world offers up glorious flavors and textures. We think it's time that everyone took full advantage of the opportunities.

CELERIAC AND CHESTNUT GRATIN WITH AMARETTO-TRUFFLE CREAM

*From Thierry Rautureau,
Chef in the Hat, Rover's*

This dish is wonderful without the truffles—but with them, it is bliss. Fresh northwest truffles, both black and white, are available in the dead of winter—January and February. Yes, they're expensive, and no, there's no real substitute. Our truffles are botanically different from the European varieties, and to firm-minded Frenchmen, they may not be considered acceptable. Yet they are every bit as earthily fragrant. Everyone describes the aroma differently; take a whiff yourself and supply your own adjective. Even if you can't afford the full tablespoon and additional slices for garnish, a small amount of fresh truffle will be worth the investment. (See Resources, page 162, for sources of local and imported truffles.)

This gratin is satisfying enough to count as a main dish for a vegetarian meal, but for omnivores it works well as a side dish to simple pan-fried steaks or chops—beef or pork are both terrific alongside.

FOR THE GRATIN:

2 CUPS HEAVY CREAM
2 TBSP AMARETTO LIQUEUR
2 CELERIAC (ABOUT 1¼ LB EACH)
SALT
FRESHLY GROUND WHITE PEPPER
6 OZ PEELED, COOKED CHESTNUTS,
    CUT INTO ⅛-INCH-THICK SLICES

FOR THE AMARETTO-TRUFFLE CREAM:

¼ CUP CRÈME FRAÎCHE
¼ CUP HEAVY CREAM
1 TBSP AMARETTO LIQUEUR
1 TBSP JULIENNED FRESH TRUFFLE

FOR THE GARNISH:

THINLY SLICED TRUFFLE
    (OPTIONAL), AS YOUR BUDGET
    ALLOWS
MINCED FRESH FLAT-LEAF PARSLEY

Serves 4
Vegetarian
Gluten-free

Make the gratin:

1 Preheat the oven to 350°F. Butter a 9-inch square baking dish. Combine the cream and amaretto in a large saucepan and bring to a boil over medium-high heat. (It's important to use a large saucepan, as the cream will bubble up quite a bit as it boils.) Reduce the heat to medium and boil until the cream is reduced by half, about 15 minutes.

2 While the cream is reducing, trim the ends from the celeriac. Set each one upright on your work surface and trim away the tough outer skin so only the tender off-white flesh remains. Halve each celeriac vertically. Use a mandoline or large sharp knife to cut it across into slices about ⅛ inch thick.

3 Arrange about one-third of the celeriac slices overlapping in the bottom of the prepared baking dish, creating as even a layer as possible. Season lightly with salt and white pepper. Scatter half the sliced chestnuts over the celeriac. Top with a layer of half the remaining celeriac, season again with salt and white pepper, and add a layer of the remaining chestnuts. Finish with the remaining celeriac slices, creating a neat layer.

Edible Tips

Celeriac has a fairly thick, tough outer rind. It's easiest to purchase the biggest knobs you can find—the texture is the same in small or large vegetables, but there's a smaller percentage of waste with the latter.

Fresh truffles are quite perishable and should be used within a few days of harvesting; same-day use is best. To store a truffle, wrap it in a paper towel and place it in the vegetable drawer; change the towel daily. Brush gently with a soft brush before cooking.

4 Slowly pour the reduced cream over the gratin, allowing it to seep down between the layers. Set the baking dish on a large rimmed baking sheet, just in case there are any drips. Cut a piece of parchment paper to cover the baking dish, generously butter the paper, and set it, butter side down, directly on top of the gratin. Bake until the celeriac is tender when pierced with the tip of a knife and the cream is mostly absorbed, about 1 hour. Remove the parchment paper about halfway through cooking, to allow the top to lightly brown.

5 Set the gratin on a wire rack to cool for at least 30 minutes before serving; it won't hold together well if served immediately. (The gratin can be made up to 1 day in advance, cut into serving portions, and reheated at 300°F for 15–20 minutes just before serving.)

Shortly before serving, make the amaretto-truffle cream:

6 Combine the crème fraîche and heavy cream in a small saucepan and warm over medium heat for about 2 minutes, whisking constantly. Add the amaretto and whisk well to froth up the sauce and thicken it slightly. Add the truffle, season to taste with salt, and keep warm over low heat.

7 To serve, cut the warm gratin into squares, then across into triangles, and carefully transfer them to individual warmed plates. Top each gratin with a few slices of truffle, slightly overlapping them. Spoon the amaretto-truffle cream around, top the gratin with a pinch of parsley, and serve right away.

ALL-DAY BAKED BEANS
WITH BACON, RUM, AND HONEY

From Jess Thomson

One of the lovely advantages to food in the Pacific Northwest is that it's not duty bound to adhere to a particular tradition. Let New Englanders battle it out over what's "correct" to add to baked beans—we can stick with what tastes great. Rockwell beans are hard to come by, but this Whidbey Island native heirloom bean is worth tracking down (see Resources, page 162). It cooks up creamy while maintaining a noticeable bite, and is the hands-down favorite bean of Whidbey Island for all baked bean preparation.

This version is the perfect dish for one of our rare snow days. Stir the ingredients together in the morning; then all you have to do for the rest of the day is peek in the oven every now and again. Add a loaf of crusty brown bread and you've got a rich and filling meal.

1 LB ROCKWELL OR RED KIDNEY BEANS, COOKED UNTIL JUST TENDER
¾ LB THICK-CUT BACON (8 SLICES), DICED
½ CUP MILD MOLASSES
½ CUP DARK RUM
2 TBSP DIJON MUSTARD
¼ TSP RED PEPPER FLAKES
½ TSP SALT
FRESHLY GROUND BLACK PEPPER
¼ CUP SPICY (SUCH AS FIREWEED OR MESQUITE) HONEY, OR TO TASTE

Serves 6
Gluten-free
Dairy-free

A day ahead of making the dish, you'll need to cook the beans:

1 Pour the beans into a colander and check them over for any stray pebbles or plant material. Rinse under cold water and pour them from the colander into a Dutch oven or stockpot. Cover completely with cold water and place the pot over medium-high heat. Bring the water to a boil and cook the beans, stirring every 45 minutes, until the beans are just tender, between 3 and 5 hours. Monitor the water level when you stir the pot, making sure the beans don't boil dry. After the first 2 hours, they can absorb water quickly, so add more than you think is necessary. Once the beans are just tender but not yet creamy inside, drain and reserve the beans. You can make the dish immediately, or refrigerate the beans overnight.

Make the dish:

2 Preheat the oven to 325°F. Place the bacon in a large, heavy, ovenproof pot, such as a cast-iron Dutch oven. Mix the beans, molasses, rum, mustard, red pepper, salt, and pepper to taste in a large bowl, and pour on top of the bacon. Carefully add water to cover the beans to about twice their depth, and bake for 2 hours, uncovered. (The liquid should be at a bare simmer.)

3 Stir; then continue to bake, checking the beans every 30 minutes or so and stirring any caramelized pieces back under, until the water is totally absorbed, the beans are plump and creamy, and the top of the dish is caramelized, for at least 3 hours and up to 8 hours. (If the beans aren't completely gooey and soft, add more water and keep cooking.)

4 Stir in the honey, taste, season with additional salt and pepper, if necessary, and serve hot. The dish can be made a day ahead and reheated before serving.

GEORGIE SMITH

Willowood Farm

When Georgie Smith talks about spilling the beans, she means it literally. She's holding a big bag of beans and attempting to pour them into a basket; if the beans get spilled, they'll bounce all over the concrete barn floor and be nearly impossible to collect. One of the fun things about hanging around farmers: you really get to visualize the roots of old sayings.

The beans at hand have a special story, one well worth spilling. They're Rockwells, with lovely pink-brown freckles, and the only place they grow in the whole world is on Whidbey Island. Georgie did some research with a vegetable historian, and from what they were able to determine, the Rockwell's roots stretch back to a common Hungarian bean colloquially referred to as "the red and white bean." It shows up in seed catalogs dating back to the 1860s. The Rockwell keeps its shape nicely when cooking, but its center develops a wonderfully creamy texture. Aside from the special local food history connection, it's a great bean for soups and baking.

Georgie's family didn't have their own private stash of Rockwell beans, as so many area farmers do. A neighbor gave her a coffee can full of seed beans in the early nineties, and she started growing them more seriously in 1995. At that point, the total worldwide production of the Rockwell was less than 300 pounds. Since then, the volume has grown to as much as 3,000 pounds between the neighboring farms. It's still nowhere near enough to keep up with demand, and Georgie and her neighbors are working hard to increase their yields and selling seed beans to interested growers.

Willowood Farm—you have to practically wade through bald eagles to get there—is in the skinny central section of Whidbey Island. These days, it's as lovely a stretch of farmland as you can find in Western Washington, but it's also the farmland that almost wasn't. In the 1970s, thanks to the combined wallop of two unexpected deaths in the family, a nationwide collapse in the viability of small farms, and a burdensome inheritance tax on the land value, Georgie's grandmother and great-aunt were making plans to sell some sandy hillside land to developers. What ensued was a nightmarish seven-year battle over property rights. In a complex serious of trades that included an official act of Congress, the National Park Service bought all but 20 acres of land from the Smiths and then sold back the land, minus the development rights, to area residents. That land is now a relatively small part of the 17,400 acres that form the Ebey's Landing National Historic Reserve.

During the years that Georgie's been farming her patch of Olympic rainshadow land, she's learned to take advantage of its relative dryness and good drainage. Unlike other nearby farms that have to cope with water-logged clay soil, her farm yields a thriving crop of garlic. The varieties that she rattles off as her favorites—Georgian Fire, Japanese, Siberian, Chesnok Red—are mind-boggling. (For garlic fans, she suggests Georgian Fire and Japanese for big roasted cloves, and Chesnok Red for everyday sauces and cooking.)

With a combined specialty in beans and garlic, it's hard not to wonder if her market stand doesn't attract more than its fair share of digestive humor. Georgie's favorite market story is even sillier—it involves a glossy cyclist pulling up to her stand and asking where to find the bananas. She, rather nicely we thought, suggested he try Florida.

GARLICKY GREENS

From R. Paul Hyman, Bin on the Lake

The fun thing about this simple dish is that it will taste a little different every time you make it, based on which greens you happen to grab from market tables. This holds true even if you use mixed greens from farms like Willie Green's or Local Roots—one week it might be red chard, young spinach, and a handful of mustard greens, but the following week it could be turnip greens instead of red chard, and radicchio instead of mustard. And don't limit yourself to spinach—explore the variety of flavors and textures available to you in quick-cooking greens.

For a lovely southern-inspired dinner, Paul serves these greens alongside Herb-Roasted Garnet Sweet Potatoes (page 36) and Brown-Sugar-Brined Pork Chops (page 63). We think they're delicious under any circumstances.

1–2 **TBSP EXTRA-VIRGIN OLIVE OIL**
2 **BUNCHES FRESH SUMMER GREENS (ABOUT 8 CUPS), WASHED AND COARSELY CHOPPED**
1–2 **CLOVES GARLIC, TO TASTE, CHOPPED**
SALT

Serves 4
Vegan
Gluten-free

1 Heat the olive oil in a large skillet over medium-high heat. Add the greens and garlic, stirring to coat with the oil. Cook until the greens are barely wilted, just a few minutes, stirring a few more times.

2 Add 2 tablespoons water and stir again, allowing the greens to steam until barely tender. Season with salt to taste and serve hot.

CREAMY PARSNIP PUREE

*From Mark Bodinet, Copperleaf
Restaurant at Cedarbrook Lodge*

These thick, pasty-white roots look like some kind of tragic carrot-farming accident, but we like to think parsnips are nature's way of helping out the parents of picky eaters. Parsnips have plenty of potassium, vitamin C, and fiber, and few kids will reject their nonthreatening appearance and sweet flavor. This sturdy vegetable is one of the last to linger on market tables at the end of the growing season; you'll find them from November through March.

Here the parsnip's natural sweetness is mellowed by the addition of cream and chicken stock, creating a surprising counterpoint to midwinter roasted or braised meat dishes. This goes beautifully with Mark's Slow-Roasted Lamb Shoulder with Preserved Huckleberries (page 66).

Edible Tip

The size and shape of your parsnips don't matter; since you'll be cooking them down to mush, any woody cores that the larger vegetables can grow don't really matter.

2 LB PARSNIPS, PEELED AND DICED
2 CUPS CHICKEN STOCK
KOSHER SALT
½ CUP HEAVY CREAM
2 TBSP UNSALTED BUTTER

Serves 4
Gluten-free

1 Place the parsnip dice in a medium saucepan with the stock. Season lightly with salt and cook over high heat until almost all the stock has evaporated, 15–20 minutes.

2 Reduce the heat to medium-low, add the cream, and simmer until it reduces by half.

3 Using an immersion blender (or carefully transfer the parsnips to a standing blender), puree the parsnips. After 30 seconds of blending, add the butter and taste to adjust the seasoning. Blend for up to 1 minute on high, until the parsnip puree is completely smooth. Serve warm.

BLASTED BROCCOLI

From Mark Fuller,
Spring Hill Restaurant

Since first tasting this broccoli at one of renowned restaurant Spring Hill's Monday Night Suppers, we've been having something of a love affair. You know how delicious French fries are. Now imagine that the best French fries in existence are made of broccoli instead of potatoes. Clearly, prayers have been answered.

These caramelized, tangy, salty florets add a whole new dimension to that dark green farmers' market staple. Officially, this is a side dish, equally delicious alongside grilled steak or juicy chicken, but on more than one occasion after a weeknight farmers' market, it's been served as a main dish, with nothing more than a bit of bread and cheese as accompaniment. When our "Recipe Box" writer Myra Kohn first cooked this, she confessed to playing "rock, paper, scissors" with her husband for the last floret. All things considered, you might want to double the recipe unless you're dining alone.

Edible Tip

Don't skip the lemon. Its acidity is what lifts the salty, caramelized florets into the realm of greatness. You might even like a bit more than half the lemon—certainly, it's better to err on the side of generosity.

2 HEADS BROCCOLI (1½ LB), CUT INTO BITE-SIZED FLORETS
¾ TSP KOSHER SALT
⅛ TSP FRESHLY GROUND BLACK PEPPER
5 TBSP EXTRA-VIRGIN OLIVE OIL
½ LEMON

Serves 2
Vegan
Gluten-free

1 Preheat the oven to 425°F. In a large bowl, toss the broccoli, salt, and pepper together with 2½ tablespoons of the olive oil. Transfer to a wire rack set in a roasting pan and roast for 10 minutes. Cool to room temperature.

2 Heat the remaining 2½ tablespoons olive oil in a 9-inch sauté pan over high heat until it starts to smoke; let it heat even a little hotter. Add the broccoli to the hot pan. Do not move it around; allow the broccoli to caramelize, cooking it for 5–8 minutes. Once one side is caramelized, stir the broccoli and try to caramelize the other sides.

3 Transfer the broccoli to a serving dish and squeeze the lemon half over it. Mix well and serve at once.

HERB-ROASTED GARNET SWEET POTATOES

From R. Paul Hyman, Bin on the Lake

Sweet potato fries have become standard pub fare for good reason: they're delicious, and the extra beta carotene is a nice bonus. These roasted sweet potatoes use savory herbs and salt to contrast with their sweetness, rather than adding ingredients that accentuate it, as is more typically seen. Because sweet potatoes are a winter vegetable, and fresh herbs don't always last in our maritime gardens through December, this recipe is easiest (and most affordable) if you have kitchen window herb pots or you're cooking it in early November, right before the first hard frost comes. If you substitute dried herbs, use the freshest, best quality you can find, and cut the amounts in half. Sage, in particular, has a different flavor when dried, so the final dish will be pretty different—although still tasty. Paul pairs these sweet potatoes with Garlicky Greens (page 33) and Brown-Sugar-Brined Pork Chops with Bacon and Maple Jus (page 63).

3 TBSP EXTRA-VIRGIN OLIVE OIL
1 TSP FRESH THYME LEAVES, MINCED
1 TSP MINCED FRESH SAGE
1 TSP MINCED FRESH OREGANO
3 MEDIUM GARNET SWEET POTATOES, PEELED AND CUT INTO ¼-INCH DICE
KOSHER SALT

Serves 4
Vegan
Gluten-free

1 Preheat the oven to 375°F. Spray a large roasting pan with nonstick cooking spray. In a large bowl, thoroughly combine the olive oil and herbs. Add the sweet potato dice to the mixture, and use your fingers to coat them well. Season with salt to taste.

2 Transfer the mixture to the prepared roasting pan. Bake for 45–60 minutes, until your desired consistency is reached, whether you like them a bit firm or fork-tender.

Edible Tip

A good alternate variety to Garnets are Red Jewels, which are easy to come by at both farmers' markets and local grocers. Look for a deep, bright color, and be sure to cook them fairly quickly after purchase—unlike potatoes, sweet potatoes don't store very well.

GREEN LENTIL SALAD

From Craig Hetherington,
Taste Restaurant

While lentils need a hotter summer than we're ever likely to see near Puget Sound, the Palouse, split between Eastern Washington and Northern Idaho, grows one-third of the country's lentils. (Pullman hosts an annual Lentil Festival in mid-August; see LentilFest.com.) The fields are striking at harvest time—lentils on the stalk are every bit as colorful as lentils in the bag. You can buy organic farm-direct French green lentils from Lentils Naturally in Fairfield (see Resources, page 162) or pick up Palouse-grown lentils from Bob's Red Mill. French green lentils hold their shape nicely during cooking, retaining a pleasantly toothsome texture. When they're properly cooked, they'll resist in about the same way properly cooked pasta does—a little bite, but no overly firm interior.

Edible Tip

If green lentils are unavailable, feel free to use Black Beluga lentils, which take slightly longer to cook, are a bit firmer, but still produce a lovely earthy flavor.

2 CUPS FRENCH GREEN LENTILS, RINSED AND PICKED OVER
4 TBSP EXTRA-VIRGIN OLIVE OIL
1 LARGE SHALLOT, JULIENNED
1 CARROT, CUT INTO SMALL DICE
PINCH OF SALT, PLUS MORE TO TASTE
1 TBSP CHOPPED FRESH THYME
1 TBSP CHOPPED FRESH PARSLEY
1–2 TBSP SHERRY VINEGAR, TO TASTE
FRESHLY GROUND BLACK PEPPER

Serves 4
Vegan
Gluten-free

1 In a large pot, cover the lentils with 2 quarts water and bring to a boil. As soon as the water comes to a boil, reduce the heat to low and simmer the lentils, checking frequently, until they are tender, 10–12 minutes. Be careful; if lentils cook too long, they will turn to mush. Drain the lentils and put in a large bowl.

2 While the lentils are cooking, heat 2 tablespoons of the olive oil in a small sauté pan over medium-low heat. Add the shallot, carrot, and salt and cook slowly until tender, 5–8 minutes.

3 Add the sautéed shallot and carrot to the lentils. Fold in the herbs, the remaining 2 tablespoons olive oil, and the vinegar until mixed well. Season with salt and pepper to taste and serve.

BLASTED SPRING VEGETABLE SALAD

From Jess Thomson

Seared in a hot oven and accessorized with a garlicky chive vinaigrette, this quick salad makes the most of spring vegetables, dressing them up a bit to bring out their crispiest textures. We cook this frequently in May and June, after stopping by the closest weeknight farmers' market. With a chunk of good cheese and a few slices of crusty bread, it's a lovely vegetarian meal all by itself (it serves 3 nicely), although we've also served it alongside grilled lamb kebabs, cold roast chicken, and even mac and cheese.

Garlic scapes were a market rarity until 2009, when the collective wisdom of farmers, chefs, and bloggers all hit critical mass, and scapes became more common and far more appreciated. Garlic bulbs send up a bright green shoot in May and June, long and skinny like a scallion, but curlier, with a pleasing garlicky flavor that is crisp and not too intense.

1 LB THICK ASPARAGUS, BOTTOMS TRIMMED AND CUT INTO 3-INCH PIECES
½ LB SUGAR SNAP OR SNOW PEAS
2 CUPS PEELED, SHELLED FAVA BEANS
¼ CUP PLUS 1 TBSP EXTRA-VIRGIN OLIVE OIL
SALT
FRESHLY GROUND BLACK PEPPER
2 TSP DIJON MUSTARD
1 OR 2 CLOVES GARLIC, TO TASTE, FINELY CHOPPED
2 TBSP CHAMPAGNE VINEGAR
⅓ CUP FINELY CHOPPED FRESH CHIVES
¼ CUP CHOPPED GARLIC SCAPES (OPTIONAL)

Serves 6
Gluten-free
Vegan

1 Preheat the oven to 500°F. Pat the asparagus, peas, and fava beans dry if necessary; then mix in a bowl with 1 tablespoon of the olive oil and salt and pepper to taste. Transfer to a baking sheet and roast until the vegetables just begin to brown and caramelize, 5–10 minutes.

2 Meanwhile, mix the mustard, garlic, and vinegar together. Whisk in the remaining ¼ cup olive oil, stir in the chives and garlic scapes, and season with salt and pepper to taste.

3 Transfer the hot vegetables to a serving platter, drizzle with the vinaigrette, and serve immediately.

Edible Tip

Peas are one of the easiest vegetables to grow at home, even if you have only a small container. Plant them early in the year—around St. Patrick's Day—and they'll be sprouting in no time. Since they love cool weather, it's one crop we can expect success with around Seattle. Tom Thumb is a fun, pint-sized variety for pot cultivation; their vines stay less than 12 inches tall. If you've got more room in the garden, try either Dwarf Grey Sugar or Lincoln for sweet peas on vines around 30 inches in height.

HEIRLOOM SUCCOTASH WITH SMOKED SALT

From Lisa Dupar

Seattle's transplanted southerners lament most loudly over our barbecue, and we aren't about to insert ourselves in the middle of a debate over properly pulled pork. Instead, we suggest a homemade picnic supper that involves Tavern Law Fried Chicken (page 69) and this salty-sweet succotash from your fellow transplant, Lisa Dupar. You'll be reaching over to the sunny side of the state for the sweet corn and lima beans, but tomatoes might be as near as your own backyard.

We hope you'll be serving cool glasses of sweet tea at your supper. And we hope you'll note that, while Seattle may lack great barbecue, we also lack mosquitoes.

Edible Tip

Not all farmers' market corn is created equal—the longer the ears sit around after they've been picked, the less sweet and creamy they'll be. A super-sweet variety is a good idea here—check with your favorite farmers—but the biggest help is buying the ears from a farm that's west of the Cascades at a weekday, not weekend, market. You'll have the best chance that it was picked the same day you'll eat it.

2 CUPS (ABOUT 1 LB) FRESH LIMA BEANS
2 TBSP EXTRA-VIRGIN OLIVE OIL
1 CUP DICED WALLA WALLA OR OTHER SWEET ONION
1 TSP CHOPPED GARLIC
¼ CUP SEEDED AND DICED POBLANO PEPPER
4 CUPS CORN SCRAPED OFF THE COB (FROM ABOUT 6 EARS), INCLUDING AS MUCH OF THE CORN CREAM AS POSSIBLE
1 CUP DICED MIXED HEIRLOOM TOMATOES
¼ CUP HEAVY CREAM
½ TSP SMOKED SEA SALT (OPTIONAL)
⅛ TSP FRESHLY GROUND BLACK PEPPER

Serves 8
Vegetarian
Gluten-free

1 Bring a medium pot of salted water to a boil. Add the lima beans and boil until almost tender, about 15 minutes. Drain.

2 In a large sauté pan over medium-low heat, warm the olive oil. Add the onion, garlic, poblano, corn and any corn cream, tomatoes, lima beans, and heavy cream. Add the smoked sea salt and pepper and cook over low heat, stirring frequently, until the corn is tender, 6–7 minutes. Serve hot.

ROASTED OZETTE POTATOES WITH CRISPY PANCETTA

From Ericka Burke,
Volunteer Park Café

This isn't just any roasted potato dish. Ozette potatoes are becoming more readily available at farmers' markets, thanks to the work of Slow Food advocates, Chefs Collaborative members, and numerous farmers. These thin-skinned fingerlings are entertainingly knobby, frequently resembling specific letters of the alphabet or the playing pieces of the old plastic Cootie game rather than the more standard oblong potato. The flavor is richer than that of many other potatoes, with a wholesome, sweet earthiness. Because Ozettes have a specific season and are still basically impossible to find outside of your own garden or a farmers' market, it's okay to substitute other fingerling potatoes here.

Edible Tip

The Ozette potato has been an ongoing project of Slow Food since 2005 and has a Northwest history going back to the late 1700s, when it was brought from Peru to the Makah tribe by Spanish missionaries. While the mission was quickly abandoned, the potato survived. If you're interested in establishing this regional heirloom in your own garden, seek out seed potatoes around March or April (see Resources, page 162).

3 LB OZETTE POTATOES
1 TBSP BLACK PEPPERCORNS
2 BAY LEAVES
8 SPRIGS FRESH THYME
½ CUP PANCETTA CUT INTO ¼-INCH DICE
SALT
FRESHLY GROUND BLACK PEPPER
2 TBSP EXTRA-VIRGIN OLIVE OIL
1 SMALL WALLA WALLA OR OTHER SWEET ONION, CUT INTO THIN JULIENNE
6 CLOVES GARLIC, THINLY SLICED
GRATED ZEST OF 1 LEMON
1 TBSP FRESH THYME LEAVES, MINCED
2 TBSP MINCED FRESH CHERVIL
2 TBSP MINCED FRESH CHIVES

Serves 6
Gluten-free
Dairy-free

1 Place the potatoes in a medium pot and cover generously with cold water. Add the peppercorns, bay leaves, and thyme sprigs. Place the pot over medium heat and gently simmer the potatoes until they are cooked through but not mushy, 15–20 minutes. Check doneness by inserting a small knife into the center of the potatoes; it should go in without any resistance. Drain; then place the potatoes on a baking sheet to cool.

2 Preheat the oven to 350°F. While the potatoes cool, heat a sauté pan over medium-high heat. Add the pancetta and cook for about 1 minute. Reduce the heat to medium and cook until crispy. Using a slotted spoon, transfer the pancetta to a paper towel–lined plate. Keep as much of the pancetta fat in the pan as possible.

3 Once the potatoes have cooled so you can handle them safely, cut them in half. Set them back on the baking sheet and spoon the reserved pancetta fat over them. Season with salt and pepper to taste. Roast the potatoes until golden brown and lightly crispy, 10–12 minutes.

4 While the potatoes are in the oven, heat the olive oil over medium-high heat in the sauté pan you used to cook the pancetta. Add the onion and garlic and sauté until translucent, 2–4 minutes. Transfer to a large serving bowl.

5 When the potatoes have finished roasting, pour them in the bowl with the onion and garlic, add the pancetta, lemon zest, and herbs, and toss until everything is well mixed. Serve hot.

CAULIFLOWER FLAN WITH PARMESAN FONDUTA AND TOASTED PINE NUT SAUCE

From Jason Stratton, Cascina Spinasse

Jason's delicious Italian food is a standout in Seattle; we expect this chef to be racking up awards for many years. And we feel a wee bit guilty for suggesting a nontraditional tweak to his *fonduta* and flans: we like to substitute Golden Glen Creamery's Parmesan for the Parmigiano-Reggiano he calls for. It's slightly less salty, but with a similar delicate nuttiness. We'd cry mea culpa, but we're smugly certain that the Italian founders of Slow Food would totally support our decision (while at the same time rolling their eyes about our flaunting of tradition). The Skagit Valley Parmesan sells out quickly, so it's not always available. In which case, we grudgingly admit to using the import. This luscious side dish is awash in rich ingredients, making it a perfect accompaniment for a lower-fat entrée. It's delicious alongside Pan-Seared Cape Cleare Coho Salmon with Marinated Fennel (page 87) or Reefnet Salmon with Salsa Verde (page 88).

FOR THE PARMESAN FONDUTA:
4 LARGE EGG YOLKS
½ TSP SUGAR
1 CUP HEAVY CREAM
4 OZ PARMESAN CHEESE, GRATED
KOSHER SALT
CAYENNE PEPPER

FOR THE TOASTED PINE NUT SAUCE:
½ CUP PINE NUTS
1 CUP CHICKEN BROTH
½ TSP GRATED LEMON ZEST
KOSHER SALT

FOR THE CAULIFLOWER FLANS:
2 HEADS CAULIFLOWER
2 TBSP EXTRA-VIRGIN OLIVE OIL
KOSHER SALT
1 CUP HEAVY CREAM
1 CUP WHOLE MILK
2 LARGE EGGS
¼ CUP FINELY GRATED PARMESAN CHEESE
FRESHLY GRATED NUTMEG
CAYENNE PEPPER

Serves 6
Gluten-free (if made with gluten-free chicken broth)

Make the Parmesan fonduta:

1 In a large bowl, whisk together the egg yolks and sugar until the yolks have lightened in color and the mixture holds a ribbon shape when the whisk is lifted. Set aside.

2 In a small sauce pot over high heat, or in a microwave-safe container in the microwave, bring the cream to a boil. Temper the egg yolks by adding the hot cream little by little to the yolks, whisking all the time, until all the cream is incorporated. Return the mixture to the pot and cook over very low heat while constantly whisking until the mixture thickens lightly. Whisk in the Parmesan a little at a time until all the cheese is incorporated and the *fonduta* is smooth. Season to taste with salt and a little cayenne. (If not using immediately, transfer to a container and press plastic wrap against the surface of the *fonduta* to prevent the formation of a skin. To reheat, heat a small amount of cream over low heat and melt the *fonduta* into it.)

Make the toasted pine nut sauce:

3 Preheat the oven to 350°F. Line a baking sheet with parchment paper and spread out the pine nuts. Toast the nuts until very deeply browned, 10–12 minutes, keeping an eye on them so they don't burn.

4 Place the toasted pine nuts, broth, and lemon zest into a small saucepan and simmer over low heat until the pine nuts are completely softened, about 1 hour. Pour the mixture into a blender and puree until very smooth. You may need to add a little bit of water to allow the mixture to spin. Season with salt to taste, and push the sauce through a fine-mesh sieve.

Meanwhile, make the cauliflower flans:

5 Increase the oven temperature to 400°F. Trim the cauliflower of their cores and leaves. Cut the cauliflower into small pieces and toss them in a large bowl with the olive oil until coated evenly. Sprinkle generously and evenly with kosher salt. Spread the cauliflower out in a single layer on a baking sheet and roast until very soft and deeply browned but not burned, 20–30 minutes.

6 Let the cauliflower cool slightly; then puree in a food processor until very smooth. Measure out 1 cup of roasted cauliflower puree and reserve the rest for another purpose. (It's delicious as a bruschetta topping, which is nice if you need a snack at this point in the cooking process.) In the food processor, combine the 1 cup puree and the cream, milk, and eggs until very smooth. Pass the mixture through a fine-mesh sieve and stir in the Parmesan. Season well with salt, a few gratings of nutmeg, and a flick of cayenne.

7 Reduce the oven temperature to 300°F. Oil 6 (4-ounce) ceramic ramekins. Ladle ½ cup of the cauliflower custard into each ramekin and gently tap it on the counter to evenly distribute. Place the ramekins in a large, flat-bottomed, shallow-sided pan and pour hot water into the pan to reach halfway up the ramekins. Cover the ramekins with a buttered sheet of parchment paper and bake until the surface of the flans feels firm to the touch, 40–45 minutes.

8 Remove the ramekins from the water and let cool slightly. These flans unmold much easier while still slightly warm.

9 To serve, unmold a flan onto each serving plate, spoon some of the warm *fonduta* on one side of the plate, and spoon some of the pine nut sauce on the other side.

SILKY KABOCHA PUREE WITH HONEY AND CARDAMOM

From Jess Thomson

Kabocha is one of the very sweetest of the winter squashes—closer to a sweet potato than an acorn squash. They look like small, squat, green-striped pumpkins, and once you know how to identify them, you'll realize that kabocha is one of the most popular varieties on late fall market tables. The skin is sturdy enough that they store nicely, so they're generally easy to find all through the winter. The flesh is nearly free of stringy squash fibers and very creamy, so you can substitute it for the Sugar Hubbard in our Sugar Hubbard Spice Loaf (page 107) or use it to make a terrific pumpkin pie. Jess originally developed this recipe as a holiday side dish, and it can easily be doubled or tripled as needed. The dish can be made several days in advance and reheated in the oven (covered) or even microwaved.

1 (3 LB) KABOCHA SQUASH
¾ TSP GROUND CARDAMOM
3 TBSP HONEY
½ TSP KOSHER SALT, OR TO TASTE
⅓ CUP VEGETABLE BROTH
2 TBSP UNSALTED BUTTER
  (OPTIONAL), CUT INTO CUBES

Serves 6
Gluten-free
Vegetarian

1 Preheat the oven to 400°F. Halve the squash, scoop out the seeds, and place, cut side up, on a parchment paper–lined baking sheet. Bake until a fork goes through the skin very easily, about 1 hour.

2 When just cool enough to handle, use a serving spoon to scrape the squash flesh out of the skins. Transfer the squash (you'll have about 6 cups) to a food processor, and whirl together with the cardamom, honey, salt, broth, and butter, if using, until extremely smooth. Taste for seasoning and serve warm.

Edible Tips

Once it's been ground, cardamom loses its complex flavor very rapidly. For the best flavor, buy whole green or white pods (the white have been bleached but are otherwise identical to the green) and grind your own right before using. Each pod is filled with very hard brown seeds; you can use either a heavy mortar and pestle or a coffee grinder.

A strong, spicy honey is a terrific accent to the pure sweet squash. Try Madrone or Golden Starthistle varieties.

GRILLED ROMANO BEANS WITH THYME AND FETA

From Jess Thomson

This is a simple, summery dish that cooks in just a few minutes. Long, flat Romano beans have a snappy crunch that is unparalleled, and tossing them on the grill (against the grates, so they don't fall right through) is an easy way of cooking them. You'll find the beans on market tables in July, peaking right around the time our summer temperatures peak. While they were rarely spotted at the markets a few years ago, they've become more common—Willie Green's, Stoney Plains, and Whistling Train stands are all good bets.

If you get a hankering for these and it's drizzly outside—with our summers, one never knows—just sauté the seasoned beans in a hot pan for a few minutes instead of grilling them. You won't lose a bit of the snap, and you'll still have the lovely Mediterranean flavors to remind you of sunny weather.

Edible Tip

If you can't find Romano beans, use fresh green beans. Adjust the cooking time down by a minute or so, to accommodate the smaller bean size.

½ LB ROMANO BEANS, ENDS
    TRIMMED
2 TSP EXTRA-VIRGIN OLIVE OIL
2 TSP CHOPPED FRESH THYME
SALT
FRESHLY GROUND BLACK PEPPER
¼ CUP CRUMBLED FETA CHEESE

Serves 4
Vegetarian
Gluten-free

1 Preheat a gas grill to medium.

2 Place the beans in a medium bowl. Drizzle with the olive oil; then sprinkle with the thyme and a bit of salt and pepper. Blend everything together with your hands until the beans are coated.

3 Transfer the beans to the cooking grate and grill for a few minutes on each side, just until bright green and marked in places.

4 Transfer to a serving plate, sprinkle with feta, and serve immediately.

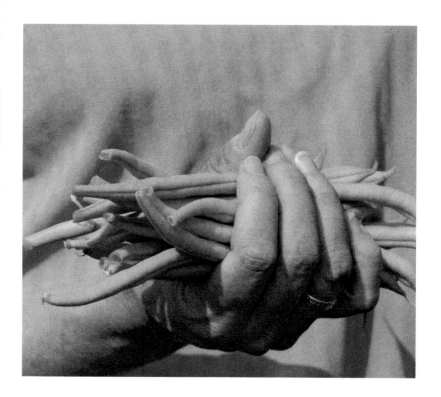

SALMON RUN VEGETABLES

From Seth Caswell, Emmer & Rye

This is vegetable perfection: a heaping mound of contrasting colors and textures, barely seasoned, and each bite a crispy, crunchy, flavorful variation on spring-time bliss. Before Seth opened Emmer & Rye, he was president of Seattle Chefs Collaborative and put in a huge number of hours helping connect farmers and fishermen with chefs and markets—and this shows every day in his cooking. All of these vegetables can be found piled on market tables from the end of April through to the end of June—hence the name. They go beautifully with Seth's recipe for Reefnet Salmon with Salsa Verde (page 88). On warm nights after a weekday market, we like to munch it down with nothing more than a hunk of good bread, a schmear of chèvre, and a glass of cold white wine.

Edible Tip

More than any other plate of vegetables in this book, we hope this inspires you to grow some of your own vegetables at home. A single zucchini vine is capable of producing all the blossoms and firm young squash you need, although we suggest far more pea vines—they're too hard to resist munching as you harvest.

1 TBSP EXTRA-VIRGIN OLIVE OIL

2 TBSP UNSALTED BUTTER

1 CLOVE GARLIC, SLICED

2 SHALLOTS, THINLY SLICED

2 BABY ZUCCHINI, HALVED LENGTHWISE AND CUT ACROSS INTO HALF MOONS

6 BABY CARROTS, THINLY SLICED ON THE BIAS

2 RADISHES, SLICED INTO ROUNDS

2 SMALL TURNIPS, SLICED INTO THIN ROUNDS

12 SUGAR SNAP PEAS, ENDS TRIMMED AND SLICED ON THE BIAS

SALT

FRESHLY GROUND BLACK PEPPER

2 CUPS SPINACH, ROUGHLY CHOPPED

8 SQUASH BLOSSOMS, STAMENS REMOVED

SPLASH OF WHITE VERJUICE OR FRESH LEMON JUICE

Serves 4
Vegetarian
Gluten-free

1 Heat a large, heavy-bottomed sauté pan over medium-high heat. Add the olive oil and 1 tablespoon of the butter, then the garlic and shallots. When the garlic and shallots become fragrant, add the zucchini, carrots, radishes, turnips, and sugar snap peas. Sauté for 2–3 minutes and watch the colors brighten. Season to taste with salt and pepper.

2 Add the spinach and sauté an additional minute or so, until the spinach wilts. Add the blossoms and allow the heat of the vegetables to wilt them. Stir in the remaining 1 tablespoon butter and the verjuice. Taste again for seasoning.

SALTY GREEN POTATO SALAD

From Jess Thomson

This is possibly the world's most addictive potato salad. Jess claims it tastes like salt-and-vinegar potato chips, but she's selling it short. Yes, it's tangy, and yes, it's salty—but it's far less intense and much more interesting than any bag of chips.

Yukon Golds are the easy choice, but as more Washington farmers grow heirloom varieties, it's fun to experiment with the unfamiliar. What matters most in this salad is the texture, as the intense dressing disguises much of the subtle potato flavor. German Butterball, Yellow Finn, and Desiree all have a pleasantly firm texture that keeps the salad from becoming mushy.

1½ LB SMALL YUKON GOLD POTATOES
2 TSP SALT
1 SHALLOT, VERY FINELY CHOPPED
¼ CUP DRAINED CAPERS, ROUGHLY CHOPPED
2 TBSP DIJON MUSTARD
¼ CUP WHITE WINE VINEGAR
¼ CUP EXTRA-VIRGIN OLIVE OIL
SALT
FRESHLY GROUND BLACK PEPPER
⅓ CUP CHOPPED FRESH CHIVES

Serves 6
Vegan
Gluten-free

1 Place the potatoes in a medium saucepan. Add cold water to cover generously and the salt, and bring to a boil. Reduce the heat to a simmer and cook until the potatoes are tender all the way through when pierced with a skewer or small knife, 15–20 minutes.

2 While the potatoes cook, whisk the shallot, capers, mustard, and vinegar together in a large bowl. Add the olive oil in a slow, steady stream, whisking to emulsify, and season to taste with salt and pepper.

3 Drain the potatoes. When cool enough to handle, slice into bite-size pieces and add to the bowl while still warm. Toss the salad to coat the potatoes well with the dressing, fold in the chives, and season again if necessary.

4 Serve warm, at room temperature, or cold the next day.

BRUCE AND SARA NAFTALY

Le Gourmand

The kitchen of Le Gourmand is tiny by professional standards, not much bigger than an average living room. Unlike in most restaurant kitchens, there are several windows around the room, adding a bit of natural light, and these windows help Bruce and Sara Naftaly cope with the otherwise less-than-excellent work space. There's also a fine selection of hand-drawn superheroes decorating a refrigerator in Sara's corner. This art gallery is the product of their son, Sam, and its existence makes the room feel even more like a home.

Bruce opened the restaurant in 1985, when Ballard was still a sleepy Scandinavian neighborhood fairly isolated from the rest of the city. Pastry chef Sara came out from New Orleans in 1998, when Bruce was still the only chef at the restaurant and made all the desserts himself. Their first date was a nettle-picking adventure, and they were engaged to be married well before Sara ever convinced Bruce to share his kitchen with her. The techniques and many of the flavors are deeply French, but the ingredients are firmly centered as close to home as possible.

Bruce's commitment to local ingredients began back in the seventies, when he became head chef at Rosellini's Other Place. In his search for quality produce, he realized that a building block of great food was establishing direct relationships with farmers. Before the Internet—before fax machines, even—he spent a lot of time on the phone, seeking out what he wanted to cook. Over the years, some of the original farmers have retired or passed away, so many of his current sources are different from the original group. In mulling over the history of his connections, Bruce mentions Whistling Train Farm because Mike Verdi's mother, Pasqualina, was an early purveyor of good vegetables at Pike Place Market and they now use Mike's farm for some produce, too. Bruce notes that their cèpes have come from the same foraging family for several generations. He's also sourced fish from University Seafood for years.

Today, much of Le Gourmand's produce is grown by the Pacific Crest School Farm. It's a few acres on Maury Island, affiliated with the Ballard-based Montessori school of the same name; Sam attends school there. They're able to make specific requests for the ingredients they're in need of—salsify, crosnes, cape gooseberries—and take advantage of the farm's unusual mix of existing trees. Before the school purchased the farmland, it belonged to an orchardist who planted many old varieties of apples, along with Asian pears, figs, cherries, and walnuts. Sara laments that with some of these varieties it's tough to know exactly what is what, so if the farm has trouble harvesting a particular Asian pear one year, it can't be easily replaced from another source. Some things from the farm, like the walnuts, weren't ingredients that they were searching for, but they have nonetheless ended up putting them to good use.

While this all might sound like a tremendous amount of effort, it's clear that for Bruce and Sara it's not. Or, more accurately, it's effort that feels worthwhile—the sort of effort that will hopefully lead to future generations of chefs taking this process for granted. At Le Gourmand, the kitchen and garden are tied together so tightly they've become inseparable. It feels right and proper and exactly how kitchens and gardens should be.

HEIRLOOM RICE SALAD

From Amy Broomhall

When blueberry-sweet red grapes are at the farmers' markets—the hot tail end of summer—you will crave this crisp, crunchy salad. This is the easy sort of summer cooking—prep the rice and tofu well ahead of time in the cool part of the day; then it's just a bit of assembly when it's too hot to stand in front of the stove. A few years ago, we discovered Eighth Wonder heirloom rice (see Resources, page 162), grown by a co-op in the Philippines that was founded by a former Seattle resident who helped build one of the city's original community gardens, in the Rainier Valley. Either their Ulikan Red or Kalinga Unoy rice will add a subtle depth to this salad. Amy—a busy mom and vocal coach who feeds a herd of growing boys—opts for the deeply nutritious bags of Mixed Grains (millet, brown rice, beans, and split peas) from Uwajimaya.

1 (12 OZ) BLOCK FIRM TOFU
1 TBSP GRAPESEED OIL
¼ CUP MIRIN
2 TBSP SESAME OIL
1 TBSP APPLE CIDER VINEGAR
3 CUPS COOKED AND COOLED
    HEIRLOOM RICE OR MIXED-
    GRAIN RICE
2 CUPS RED GRAPES, HALVED
4 SCALLIONS, THINLY SLICED
1 RED BELL PEPPER, SEEDED AND
    THINLY SLICED

SALT
FRESHLY GROUND BLACK PEPPER
¾ CUP RAW OR SALTED OR
    ROASTED CASHEWS

Serves 4
Vegan
Gluten-free (if made with heirloom rice, not with mixed grains)

1 Heat a large sauté pan over medium-high heat. Slice the tofu into ⅓-inch-thick slabs. Add the grapeseed oil to the hot pan and fry the tofu until it is golden brown, about 4 minutes per side. Remove from the pan and let cool. Slice the fried tofu into small strips.

2 Whisk together the mirin, sesame oil, and vinegar in a small bowl for the dressing. Set aside.

3 In a large salad bowl, gently toss the cooked rice, grape halves, scallions, pepper slices, and fried tofu strips together. Fold in the dressing and season to taste with salt and pepper.

4 Add the cashews just before serving (they will get soft and rubbery if allowed to sit).

Edible Tip

In the small town of Prosser, AprèsVin (ApresVin.com) makes grapeseed oils from the Yakima Valley wine grapes—not only can you find a range of oil types based on varietal, their process utilizes grapes after they've been pressed for wine, making it a sound environmental choice. Their Chardonnay and Riesling oils are great choices for this salad.

SAUSAGE AND WINTER GREENS GRATIN

From Jess Thomson

Jess originally created this dish as a side for a big holiday feast. Doubled, it still works perfectly for that. During our muddy trudge of winter-into-spring, it's one of the few dishes that can still be picked up entirely at the farmers' market. Kale and chard abound on the produce tables, and Golden Glen makes a Parmesan that works well here. Stop by Skagit River Ranch for some Italian sausage and you're set.

Another good thing about this gratin is what it does for the dark leafy green bugaboos. People who swear they don't like kale have happily munched down a double helping. Don't worry too much about the overall mix of greens. As long as you're using big, tough leaves built for braising, the gratin will turn out fine.

Edible Tip

Subbing in chicken sausage is fine (we've had good results with both Uli's and Isernio's), but you'll need to add a touch more olive oil to compensate for the lower fat content of the meat.

½ LB SWEET OR HOT BULK ITALIAN
  SAUSAGE
½ LB GREEN CHARD
½ LB LACINATO (DINOSAUR) KALE
½ LB COLLARD GREENS
2 TSP EXTRA-VIRGIN OLIVE OIL
½ CUP CHICKEN BROTH
SALT
FRESHLY GROUND BLACK PEPPER

2 TSP ALL-PURPOSE FLOUR
2 TSP UNSALTED BUTTER,
  CUT INTO SMALL PIECES
¼ CUP GRATED PARMESAN CHEESE
⅓ CUP HEAVY CREAM

Serves 4

1 Preheat the oven to 375°F. Butter an 8-inch square baking dish.

2 Heat a large, heavy soup pot over medium heat. Add the sausage and cook, breaking it up into bite-size pieces as you go, until it is no longer pink, about 8 minutes. Using a slotted spoon, remove the sausage to a paper towel–lined plate. Reserve any sausage drippings in the pot.

3 Meanwhile, cut the tough center ribs out of all the greens, slice the leaves into ¼-inch-wide ribbons, and wash and dry them in a salad spinner.

4 Add the olive oil to the sausage drippings, and then starting adding the greens, about a third of them at first, then adding the rest in batches as what's in the pan cooks down. When all the greens have been added, stir for about 5 minutes, until they have all begun to soften. Add the broth, cover the pot, and cook for 10 minutes, stirring once or twice.

5 Take the lid off and cook another 10 minutes or so, until almost no liquid remains at the bottom of the pot. (You want the greens to be fairly dry. If you still have extra liquid after 15 minutes, just scoop it out.) Season the greens to taste with salt and pepper.

6 Remove the pot from the heat, add the sausage, and stir in the flour until no white remains. Transfer the mixture to the prepared baking dish and even out the top with a rubber spatula. Dot the mixture with the butter, sprinkle with the Parmesan, and drizzle the cream over the whole thing. Bake until the cream is bubbling and the cheese is browned, about 30 minutes. Serve warm or at room temperature.

SIMPLE BRAISED BRUSSELS SPROUTS

From Mark Bodinet, Copperleaf Restaurant at Cedarbrook Lodge

Brussels sprouts have been rescued from the compost heap forever, thanks to farm-to-table chefs showing us once and for all that this midwinter vegetable can be delicious. If nothing else, they're a welcome break from kale! Brussels sprouts are easy to find from any number of Western Washington row crop farmers. For the first two weeks in the season (generally early November), they're barely bite-size, and if yours are that small, you'll need to both up the quantity here and reduce the cooking time, lest you go hungry and they turn mushy. Typically, though, an average Brussels sprout will be an oval about an inch across and 2 inches long. The short braise in chicken stock gives them flavor while keeping their dense, crunchy texture. Mark Serves these with his Vanilla-Scented Sweet Potato Puree (page 57) and Rabbit with Honey-Poached Cranberries and Dijon Sauce (page 60). They're also great alongside a basic roast chicken.

Edible Tip

There's absolutely no reason you couldn't substitute a good vegetable stock if you'd rather go vegetarian, but we do suggest one that's free of tomatoes. Not only can it tint the sprouts slightly pink, but the extra acidity isn't a flavor you want here.

1 TBSP UNSALTED BUTTER
10 BRUSSELS SPROUTS, CUT IN HALF
1 CUP CHICKEN STOCK
KOSHER SALT

Serves 2–4
Gluten-free

1 Preheat the oven to 375°F.

2 In a large, oven-safe sauté pan, melt the butter over high heat; then carefully add the Brussels sprouts, cut side down, in a single layer. Slowly pour in the stock and season to taste with salt. Place the pan in the oven until the sprouts are tender, about 10 minutes. Serve hot.

BROWNED BRAISED BABY TURNIPS

From Bruce Naftaly, Le Gourmand

A few years ago, baby turnips started appearing on the market tables of free-wheeling vegetable farmers and occasionally in CSA boxes. We got a lot of questions about how they should be cooked, as the turnip of most people's experience is tough, the size of a softball, and not very appealing. These pearly treats are most common in June, but as they've become more popular, farmers are varying their planting times and we've seen them as early as April and as late as October. At Le Gourmand, Bruce Serves these turnips with roast duck, but they're equally delicious with roast chicken or pork. If your stock isn't homemade, be sure to choose a low-sodium kind or the final dish will almost certainly be too salty. Also, don't shy away from the three kinds of alcohol. We've teased Bruce about his tendency to add cognac to almost everything he cooks, but the delicious results are worth every drop.

Edible Tip

If you can't find baby turnips, larger ones can be used as long as they're peeled and cut into smaller pieces. The basic turnip flavor will be a little stronger, but the glaze is flavorful enough to stand up to it.

1 TBSP UNSALTED BUTTER

24 BABY (ABOUT 1 INCH IN DIAMETER) TURNIPS, TRIMMED

2 CUPS STOCK (CHICKEN, DUCK, OR VEGETABLE)

½ CUP MADEIRA

¼ CUP COGNAC

¼ CUP PORT

SALT

FRESHLY GROUND BLACK PEPPER

Serves 4
Vegetarian (if made with vegetable stock)
Gluten-free

1 In a heavy-bottomed nonreactive sauté pan big enough to cook the turnips in a single layer, melt the butter over medium-high heat. Add the turnips and sauté until lightly browned, about 5 minutes.

2 Add the stock, Madeira, cognac, and port. Bring to a boil; then lower the heat to a simmer. Cover and simmer until almost all the liquid has evaporated, about 20 minutes.

3 Roll the turnips around in the pan to coat them with the delicious glaze. Season with salt and pepper to taste. Serve immediately.

SPICED ROASTED SPUD NUTS

From Jess Thomson

These salty-sweet potatoes are as easy to munch your way through as a bowl of popcorn. Olsen Farms sells adorable "spud nuts," which are multicolored new potatoes about an inch in diameter (they get slightly larger as the growing season progresses at the farm in Colville). Because the potato skins get thoroughly crusted with the spice rub, the color doesn't come through very much, so the more easily available Yukon Golds will also serve nicely.

Prep time is quickest when potatoes are less than an inch in diameter—you can just rinse them off and start cooking. If all you find are larger potatoes—small ones are most common on market tables in early summer—cut them into big bite-size chunks. They're especially great with lamb burgers or souvlaki.

1 LB SMALL NEW POTATOES
1 TBSP EXTRA-VIRGIN OLIVE OIL
1 TSP KOSHER SALT
1 TSP GROUND CUMIN
½ TSP GROUND CORIANDER
¼ TSP GROUND CINNAMON
FRESHLY GROUND BLACK PEPPER

Serves 4
Vegan
Gluten-free

1 Preheat the oven to 425°F.

2 Toss the potatoes with the olive oil in a large bowl. Mix the salt, cumin, coriander, and cinnamon together in a small bowl, sprinkle evenly over the potatoes, and mix with your hands until the spices are evenly distributed.

3 Transfer the potatoes to a baking dish large enough so the potatoes can sit in a single layer, season to taste with pepper, and roast until cooked through, 20–25 minutes. Serve warm or at room temperature.

SUNCHOKE AND CHANTERELLE HASH

From Martin Woods,
Re: public Restaurant & Bar

This hash is full of nicely contrasting textures and rich fall flavor. Sunchokes, also called Jerusalem artichokes, are a North American native, loaded with fiber and having a mild, slightly nutty flavor. When they're combined with meaty chanterelles and chewy kale ribbons—all available on farmers' market tables throughout October—this is a great side dish for the last outdoor-grilled steak of the season.

When it comes to choosing kale, our default is lacinato—sometimes called dinosaur kale. It has narrow, blue-green, densely rippled leaves and a mild flavor. It also happens to be the variety that avowed kale haters (they are legion) will happily eat. Once you get the hang of slicing out their thick stalks, kale doesn't really take any more prep time than other vegetables, and it's so loaded with calcium and a long list of vitamins that it really is worth learning to love it.

1 LARGE BUNCH KALE
4 TSP UNSALTED BUTTER
½ TSP OLIVE OIL
1 LB WASHED SUNCHOKES, CUT INTO 1-INCH PIECES ON A SLANT
½ LB CHANTERELLES
2 SHALLOTS, THINLY SLICED
¾ CUP VEGETABLE STOCK
¾ TSP FRESH THYME LEAVES
FRESH LEMON JUICE
SEA SALT
FRESHLY GROUND BLACK PEPPER

Serves 4
Vegetarian
Gluten-free

1 Fill a stockpot halfway with water, and bring to a boil. While you're waiting for the water to boil, rinse the kale and remove their thick stems with a sharp paring knife. Plunge the destemmed leaves into the boiling water and let them cook about a minute, until they're nicely wilted. Remove from the pot with tongs, turn off the heat, and once the kale leaves are cool enough to handle, slice the blanched leaves into short ribbons. Set aside.

2 Warm 2 teaspoons of the butter and the olive oil together in a large sauté pan over medium heat. Add the sunchokes and cook until browned on one side, about 8 minutes. Add the chanterelles and gently stir until they begin to brown and the sunchokes have caramelized on all sides, another 6–8 minutes. Add the shallots and cook for 1–2 minutes.

3 Add the kale and toss until well mixed; then pour in the stock and reduce the heat to low. Cook until the stock has reduced by 60–70 percent. Add the remaining 2 teaspoons butter and continue cooking and stirring until the butter is combined with the reduced stock. Remove from the heat and add the thyme. Season with lemon juice, salt, and pepper to taste, and serve.

Edible Tips

Sunchokes are native to the eastern seaboard, but these days Washington is responsible for a substantial percentage of those grown in the United States. They look like a cross between a fingerling potato and a gingerroot—bumpy, with a thin, crackly skin. They can bruise easily, so check them over at purchase to avoid those with soft spots.

Both the texture and the flavor of the chanterelles are an important part of the dish. If you want to spend less money, we suggest using fewer chanterelles rather than substituting a different kind.

VANILLA-SCENTED SWEET POTATO PUREE

From Mark Bodinet, Copperleaf
Restaurant at Cedarbrook Lodge

We are on a mission regarding these sweet, nutritious tubers: yam and sweet potato are not interchangeable words, regardless of what the signs imply in your nearest produce department. Yams are a tropical vine and their tubers can grow many feet in length. You will only rarely find them around Seattle at an international grocery, and unless our climate changes drastically or a farmer builds a very expensive greenhouse, you will not find them grown in Washington. Everything else— pale yellow, bright orange, or somewhere in between—is a sweet potato, which is a member of the morning glory family. Many sweet potato varieties grow beautifully in these parts; they start appearing at farmers' markets in early fall. We find the best flavor and texture in the brighter varieties, like Garnet and Red Jewel.

This spicy-sweet puree goes beautifully with Mark's Rabbit with Honey-Poached Cranberries and Dijon Sauce (page 60).

1 LB GARNET SWEET POTATOES, PEELED AND DICED
1 VANILLA BEAN, SPLIT IN HALF
1 (2-INCH) CINNAMON STICK, FRESHLY GROUND
1 WHOLE CLOVE, GROUND
1 ALLSPICE BERRY, GROUND

2 CUPS CHICKEN STOCK
KOSHER SALT
½ CUP HEAVY CREAM
2 TBSP UNSALTED BUTTER

Serves 4
Gluten-free

1 Place the sweet potato dice, vanilla, and spices in a medium saucepan with the stock. Season lightly with salt. Bring to a boil and cook over high heat until almost all the stock has evaporated, about 25 minutes. Add the cream and simmer until it reduces by half, 10 minutes. Remove and discard the vanilla bean.

2 Carefully transfer the mixture to a blender and start to process, first on low, then gradually increasing the speed to high. Once on high, pause, add the butter, and taste to check the seasoning. Blend on high until the puree is completely smooth, about 1 minute. Serve warm.

Edible Tips

Use either a mortar and pestle or small coffee grinder to grind your spices fresh—or just use ¾ teaspoon good-quality cinnamon and generous pinches of ground cloves and allspice. Check World Spice Merchants for four types of cinnamon (see Resources, page 162).

We always opt for Mexican vanilla beans rather than the more popular Madagascar varieties. This is partly because we like supporting the vanilla orchid in its original native country, partly because we think they have a more straightforward vanilla intensity, and partly because we figure it saves on fossil fuel.

CHAPTER 3

MAIN DISHES

Seattle has never been a boring meat 'n' potatoes city. Why should we be, when our town stretches between two of the best shellfish beaches in creation, when we're home to the world's greatest salmon, when our chefs have an equal love of Pacific Rim condiments and fresh herbs from their own gardens? Whether the focus is fresh tofu from the International District, mussels from the Totten Inlet, lamb from Colville, or paneer from Ferndale, these recipes make the best possible use of delectable local protein. You will find one rather lonely meat 'n' potatoes recipe here—a very traditional French dish that makes use of a rather obscure cut of beef. It is anything but boring, which is just how it should be. When Seattle does eat meat 'n' potatoes, we expect greatness.

RABBIT WITH HONEY-POACHED CRANBERRIES AND DIJON SAUCE

From Mark Bodinet, Copperleaf Restaurant at Cedarbrook Lodge

Stokesberry Sustainable Farm has long been beloved for its flavorful chickens and gorgeous eggs, and since the summer of 2011, its been providing fat, tender rabbits to its farmers' market customers, too. It's been several generations since most Americans cooked rabbits at home—and it's still fairly unusual to find on menus outside of French or Moroccan restaurants. Rabbit is strikingly lean, and farm-raised rabbit is quite mild, with a subtle sweetness—similar to great pork tenderloin. Its mild flavor is set off here with tangy-sweet honeyed cranberries and a Dijon sauce. Mark pairs the rabbit with Simple Braised Brussels Sprouts (page 53) and Vanilla-Scented Sweet Potato Puree (page 57).

FOR THE HONEY-POACHED CRANBERRIES:
½ CUP HONEY
½ CUP FRESH CRANBERRIES, PICKED OVER

FOR THE DIJON SAUCE:
2 TBSP EXTRA-VIRGIN OLIVE OIL
1 CARCASS FROM A ROASTED 2 LB CHICKEN, BROKEN INTO PIECES
2 CARROTS, CHOPPED
1 YELLOW ONION, CHOPPED
2 SPRIGS FRESH THYME
2 CUP RED WINE
2 CUPS CHICKEN STOCK
½ CUP DIJON MUSTARD
2 TBSP UNSALTED BUTTER

FOR THE RABBIT:
4 RABBIT LEGS
KOSHER SALT
FRESHLY GROUND BLACK PEPPER
4 SPRIGS FRESH THYME
4 CLOVES GARLIC, PEELED
2 CUPS CHICKEN STOCK
4 RABBIT LOINS
2 TBSP EXTRA-VIRGIN OLIVE OIL
2 TBSP UNSALTED BUTTER
FLEUR DE SEL

Serves 4

Make the honey-poached cranberries:

1 In a small sauté pan over high heat, bring the honey to a boil; then immediately remove from the heat. Add the cranberries, stir to coat with the honey, and cover. Keep warm until ready to serve.

Make the Dijon sauce:

2 Heat a large saucepan over high heat. Add the olive oil and chicken carcass bones and sauté until golden brown on all sides. Season to taste with salt and pepper. Add the carrot, onion, and thyme and cook until lightly browned.

3 Remove the pan from the heat and add the wine. Return the pan to the heat and simmer until the wine is reduced by half, 10–15 minutes. Add the stock and mustard and turn the heat to low. Gently simmer for 5 minutes. Strain the sauce from the bones through a fine mesh sieve and return to the pan. Whisk in the butter and keep the sauce warm.

This dish calls for a high-acid varietal such as Sangiovese (the noble grape of Tuscany) or Grenache (commonly grown in France's Southern Rhone). Bob Betz, winemaker at Betz Family Winery, combines Italian winemaking philosophy with French varietals to craft the '09 Besoleil, made of Grenache and a touch of Syrah and Mouvedre. Rabbit can be lean and gamey, making it a natural pairing for a fruity Grenache, while the lipsmacking acidity of the Besoleil neutralizes the richness of the dish.

Cook the rabbit:

4 Preheat the oven to 375°F. Season the rabbit legs with salt and pepper. Over high heat in a large oven-safe sauté pan, sear the legs on all sides until golden brown. Add 2 sprigs of the thyme, two garlic cloves, and the stock. Place the pan in the oven until the legs are tender, about 20 minutes. Remove the legs from the pan and keep them warm.

5 Heat a medium-size sauté pan over high heat. Season the loins with salt and pepper on all sides. Add the olive oil to the pan. When the pan is hot, carefully place the loins in it and sear on all sides until golden brown. Add the butter and the remaining 2 sprigs thyme and 2 cloves garlic, and remove the pan from the heat. Let the rabbit simmer in the butter, off the heat, for 1 minute to finish cooking.

6 To serve, transfer one leg and one loin to each plate. Drizzle generously with the Dijon sauce and accompany with several tablespoons of the cranberries. Season with fleur de sel and freshly ground pepper.

MARK BODINET

Copperleaf Restaurant at Cedarbrook Lodge

Picture this: near SeaTac airport and just off the freeway sits a modest concrete hotel. Now erase that mental picture, because Cedarbrook Lodge is not remotely like any of the other countless hotels that fit that description. It perches next to a wetland, surrounded by an array of native species and quiet walking paths. It has an onsite farm, complete with mushroom garden, water reclamation system, and food-composting program. Its Copperleaf Restaurant manages to be simultaneously cozy (there's a big fireplace and a good amount of space between tables) and grand (huge windows overlooking the wetlands, soaring ceilings). It sure doesn't feel like you're next to the airport.

Mark Bodinet is the lucky, and seriously dedicated, chef at Copperleaf; he's from Chicago originally and came to Seattle via Martha's Vineyard and Napa Valley. More accurately, he came here via Roy Breiman, the hotel's culinary director. Roy first hired Mark straight out of culinary school in Arizona to come work with him as chef de partie at a seasonal boutique hotel on Martha's Vineyard; Mark worked the fish station. When Roy moved on to Salish Lodge, Mark followed him for a brief stint. Then, thanks in part to Roy's letter

of recommendation to Thomas Keller, Mark moved on to five years at The French Laundry. Mark describes Roy as a mentor, but at this point in their careers there's a clear degree of collaboration that comes through. Roy handles everything from finding the best local sources for ingredients to planning the chef's garden to shifting all the disposable cutlery used by the hotel to compostable products. Mark is found mainly in the kitchen, executing their shared locally sourced vision.

It's not uncommon for dedicated chefs to have their own kitchen gardens, but Copperleaf's mushroom garden is possibly unique in the region. The grounds have a water reclamation project, where they get the water for the vegetable garden. Mushrooms are a terrific natural filtration system, so they planted a bed of Brandywine mushroom spores, with a layer of straw mulch to help keep the temperature fluctuations to a minimum. They're able to use these mushrooms during the summer months—Mark says they look like porcini but have their own distinct flavor—but the spores function as water filtration year-round. There are also four substantial raised beds for seasonal produce. The entire kitchen crew, including a few staff

members with farming backgrounds, works in the gardens.

As for their local sourcing, you'll spot plenty of the usual names—Fishing Vessel St. Jude for albacore tuna, Bluebird Grain Farms for emmer, World Spice for any number of seasonings—but as with the mushroom garden, there are some unusual things afoot. First is Bernie Nash of Mad Hatcher Farm in Ephrata, who not only provides the eggs but raises squab, poussin, chicken, and rabbit for the kitchen. While plenty of Seattle kitchens have locally sourced chickens and eggs on the menu, California is the more typical source for the squab and rabbit. All the bacon and prosciutto are house-cured, using Eastern Washington pigs.

Talking about an occasional source of annoyance to locavores—the perception that "local" doesn't always mean "the most delicious"—Mark just says that for him, "best" and "as local as possible" are essentially the same thing. That's the goal: a menu where "local" and "best" interact naturally, reflecting the seasons, the technique, and the talents of small farmers. Mark achieves that goal with ease, bringing equal pleasure to himself and his lucky diners.

BROWN-SUGAR-BRINED PORK CHOPS
WITH BACON AND MAPLE JUS

From R. Paul Hyman, Bin on the Lake

Any lover of pork likely came to a screeching halt at that title. A great pork chop, not overcooked and served plain, is tasty enough—especially with sweet whey-fed pork from the Skagit Valley. The combination of our burgeoning cheese industry and our small polyculture farms is a most serendipitous one: pigs love the whey, and cheesemakers are happy it doesn't go to waste. Samish Bay even keeps the process entirely on the farm; remember to pick up a wedge of their aged Ladysmith cheese when stopping by their market stand for a bone-in pork roast. For the bacon, Paul suggests applewood smoked, but we are betting you've got a favorite supplier already. Thick-cut is important, so it won't overcook. Paul serves these pork chops with Herb-Roasted Garnet Sweet Potatoes (page 36). The combination is a delectably salty-sweet riff on southern food that feels strangely at home in our northern latitudes. You'll need to start this recipe 24 hours ahead.

Edible Wine Pairing

**2007 VA PIANO SYRAH,
COLUMBIA VALLEY, $40**

This very masculine dish begs for a masculine wine, and the '07 Va Piano Syrah, Columbia Valley, delivers with a muscular punch. Classic Syrah qualities of blueberries and plum make for a natural pairing with pork. Minerals and smoke lift the heavy bacon and maple flavors of the dish.

FOR THE PORK CHOPS:
2 TBSP FENNEL SEEDS
1 TBSP BLACK PEPPERCORNS
1 TSP WHOLE CLOVES
4 DRIED BAY LEAVES
4 CLOVES GARLIC
¾ CUP FIRMLY PACKED BROWN
   SUGAR
¾ CUP KOSHER SALT
1 (4-BONE) PORK RACK
KOSHER SALT
FRESHLY GROUND BLACK PEPPER
2 TBSP CANOLA OIL

2 TBSP UNSALTED BUTTER,
   CUT INTO 2 PATS
4 SLICES THICK-CUT BACON
   (ABOUT ½ INCH THICK AND
   5 INCHES LONG)

FOR THE MAPLE JUS:
1 CUP PURE MAPLE SYRUP
2 CUPS PORK STOCK
1 TSP SHERRY VINEGAR

Serves 4

1 In a large saucepan over medium-high heat, toast the fennel seeds, peppercorns, and cloves for 2 minutes. Add the bay leaves, garlic, and 1 cup water and bring to a boil. Stir in the brown sugar and salt and stir to dissolve, about 2 minutes. Remove from the heat, add ½ gallon cold water, and place in a container big enough to hold the brine plus the fully submerged pork rack. Add the pork and refrigerate overnight.

2 The next day, preheat the oven to 350°F. Remove the pork from the brine and pat dry. Season with salt and pepper (remember that the bacon will add extra saltiness to the finished dish) and place it, loin side down, in a flameproof roasting pan. Set the pan over a large burner on medium-high heat and add the canola oil. Sear the pork for 3 minutes; then remove the pan from the heat. Turn the rack over, so it's bone side down. Place the 2 pats of butter on top of the loin side. Place the pan in the oven and roast until the internal temperature is 135–140°F, 20–25 minutes.

3 While the pork is roasting, render the bacon in a sauté pan over low heat, about 4 minutes per side, until it's crisp on the outside but still tender on the inside. To make the maple jus, in a small, heavy saucepan over low heat, combine the maple syrup and stock. Reduce the mixture until you have 1 cup of thick sauce, about 25–30 minutes. Stir in the vinegar. Remove from the heat but keep warm.

4 Remove the roast from the oven and let rest for 8–10 minutes; then slice near the bones for 4 portions. Place one pork chop on each plate, and drape a slice of bacon over the top. Drizzle the maple jus on the chop and bacon and serve.

CIDER-BRAISED PORK
WITH APPLES, ONIONS, AND THYME

This is a quintessential Seattle autumn dish, made to be eaten with a bowl of mashed potatoes, accompanied with a bottle of hard cider, and finished off with a slice of apple pie (and possibly a nap). Most of the pork from our local farms is mild, with a clean flavor that shines through the rich braising liquid. If you want a more intensely porky experience, look for the Mangalitsa pigs raised by Heath Putnam Farms; he sells at the University District Farmers' Market. This Austrian breed has thick, wooly coats and the ability to layer on fat like few other breeds; its foraging habit and natural characteristics lead to meat that is richer and darker, with pronounced flavor notes that the typical Berkshire-cross pig raised by other farms simply can't provide.

Edible Tip

To peel pearl onions, trim off the root strings with a small knife and score the bottom of the onion with a small X. Blanch in boiling water for 2 minutes; then refresh under cold water, and peel.

2 TBSP ALL-PURPOSE FLOUR
SALT
FRESHLY GROUND BLACK PEPPER
1 (2¾ LB) TIED PORK SHOULDER ROAST, NETTING OR STRING INTACT
1 TBSP PEANUT OR VEGETABLE OIL, PLUS MORE, IF NEEDED
1 TBSP OLIVE OIL
2 MEDIUM LEEKS, HALVED LENGTHWISE AND CUT INTO HALF-MOONS
2 CLOVES GARLIC, FINELY CHOPPED
½ LB SMALL YELLOW PEARL ONIONS, PEELED
1 TBSP CHOPPED FRESH THYME
3–4 CUPS HARD APPLE CIDER
1 TART APPLE, PEELED, CORED, AND CUBED
1 TBSP DIJON MUSTARD
1 TBSP CHOPPED FRESH FLAT-LEAF PARSLEY

Serves 6
Dairy-free
Gluten-free (if made with gluten-free cider)

1 Preheat the oven to 325°F. Heat a large, heavy, ovenproof soup pot or Dutch oven (with a tight-fitting lid) over medium-high heat. Place the flour on a small plate. Season the flour liberally with salt and pepper. Pat the pork dry; then coat it on all sides with the flour mixture.

2 When the pot is hot, add the peanut oil and sear the pork (leaving the string on) until nicely browned on all sides, 3–4 minutes per side. Transfer the pork to a plate, and carefully wipe the pot clean with paper towels. Reduce the heat to medium.

3 Add the olive oil to the pot, then the leeks, and cook, stirring, for 3 minutes. Add the garlic, onions, and thyme, and season with salt and pepper. Cook and stir for 2 minutes, then nestle the pork in among the vegetables. Add the cider until it comes about halfway up the sides of the pork, cover the pot, and transfer it to the oven. Braise for 1 hour; then turn the pork over, add the apple cubes, and braise for another hour or so, until the pork yields completely when poked with a skewer.

4 Transfer the pork to a platter, cover with foil, and let rest. Meanwhile, return the braising liquid to the stove top, and simmer until considerably thickened, about 15 minutes. Stir in the mustard; then season to taste with salt and pepper. Stir in the parsley.

5 Slice the pork and top with the apples, vegetables, and braising liquid.

Edible Cider Pairing

Washington's hard cider is experiencing a delicious renaissance as orchards around the state return to planting cider apples and older heirloom varieties. See Resources, page 162, for a selection of our favorite local ciders that would work wonderfully with this dish, either to cook with or sip alongside:

Alpenfire: This certified organic and gluten-free cidery makes a *méthode champenoise* cider named Flame that's lovely for pairing, although the bubbles are lost in cooking. For the braising liquid, try their Spark Bittersweet, which uses classic French cider apples.

Finnriver: Their festive Méthode Ancestrale sparkling cider is a perfect pairing with this braised pork. It is pure apple flavor with plenty of fizz.

Red Barn: Don't be misled by the name Sweetie Pie. This blend is made with lots of Gravensteins and has a complex flavor that's great for both the braising liquid and to pair with the finished dish.

Rockridge Orchards: We suggest rich, slightly sweet Quarry Stone for cooking and crisp Cobblestone for drinking. Wade Bennett also makes a splendidly smooth aged apple brandy, which would be perfect to serve in a snifter after dinner.

Snowdrift: Their Cliffbreaks Blend is the one to choose for either cooking or pairing with this dish—its strong tannins and balanced flavors will stand up beautifully.

Tieton Ciderworks: Wild Washington Apple has a fine balance between crisply acidic and apple-y sweetness. Its light carbonation makes it nice for pairing.

SLOW-ROASTED LAMB SHOULDER
WITH PRESERVED HUCKLEBERRIES

*From Mark Bodinet, Copperleaf
Restaurant at Cedarbrook Lodge*

Most of our local lamb-loving chefs, including Mark, use Anderson Ranch lamb from Oregon. Yes, it's delicious, but so is the incredibly mild lamb raised by Olsen Farms out in Colville. (Brent Olsen is more famous for his potatoes than for his lamb or beef, but it's all fantastic, and the combination should make obvious why we call him the Stew Farmer.) For a minerally touch of maritime flavor in the meat, the lamb from Lopez Island Farm is luscious. Or, for a unique opportunity to support The Evergreen State College's sustainable agriculture program, you can buy student-raised lamb quarters from Olympia (see Resources, page 162). The perfect textural and flavor accompaniment for this dish is Mark's Creamy Parsnip Puree (page 34).

Edible Wine Pairing

**2007 CADENCE BEL CANTO, CARA MIA
VINEYARD, RED MOUNTAIN, $60**

A blend of about two-thirds Cabernet Franc and one-third Merlot with a touch of Petit Verdot, all from the Cadence Winery's estate vineyard, Cara Mia. The baking spices, herbs, and minerality from the Cabernet Franc are like seasoning for lamb, while the layers of black fruit marry the preserved huckleberries.

FOR THE LAMB:
1 (2 LB) LAMB SHOULDER
KOSHER SALT
FRESHLY GROUND BLACK PEPPER
3 TBSP EXTRA-VIRGIN OLIVE OIL
2 SHALLOTS, PEELED BUT LEFT
    WHOLE
1 BULB GARLIC, CUT IN HALF
1 BUNCH FRESH THYME

FOR THE PRESERVED
HUCKLEBERRIES:
½ CUP RED WINE VINEGAR
¾ CUP SUGAR

1½ TSP ALLSPICE
1½ TSP STAR ANISE
1 (3- TO 4-INCH) CINNAMON STICK
1 TBSP GROUND CORIANDER
1 FRESH BAY LEAF
1 TBSP BLACK PEPPERCORNS
2 CUPS FRESH PURPLE
    HUCKLEBERRIES
FLEUR DE SEL
FRESHLY GROUND BLACK PEPPER

Serves 4
Gluten-free
Dairy-free

Make the lamb:

1 Preheat the oven to 300°F. Season the lamb shoulder liberally with salt and pepper and place in an oven-safe casserole dish with a tight-fitting lid. Pour the olive oil over the seasoned lamb and the add shallots, garlic, and thyme to the dish.

2 Cover and cook until very tender, about 3½ hours.

Make the preserved huckleberries:

3 In a medium saucepan over medium heat, combine 2 cups water and the vinegar and sugar, and stir well. Add the allspice, star anise, cinnamon stick, coriander, bay leaf, and peppercorns and stir gently to combine. Cook the spiced liquid until the total volume is reduced by two-thirds, about 12 minutes.

4 Remove the pan from the heat and let stand at room temperature for 10 minutes. Carefully strain the spices out. Add the huckleberries, stirring gently to combine.

5 To serve, carefully remove the lamb from the casserole. Divide evenly among four plates. Season to taste with fleur de sel and pepper and spoon over the huckleberry sauce.

FEISTY CHICKEN KARAAGE

Adapted by Sumi Hahn

Boneless, well-seasoned dark meat and an incredibly delicate gluten-free coating: this Japanese version of fried chicken is possibly even more addictive than the southern version. If you feel inspired to decide this once and for all, our Tavern Law Fried Chicken recipe (page 69) is more than ready to go thigh to thigh with *karaage*. You can find great chicken thighs from Stokesberry Sustainable Farm or Skagit River Ranch, although you'll have to do the boning and skinning yourself. (No worries, it can all go straight into the city yard waste bins.) Bob's Red Mill is the most easily available brand of potato starch, although you'll find a few other varieties at Uwajimaya and Viet Wah. Make sure you get the starch, and not the flour—while both are from potatoes, the final cooked texture is quite different. *Note:* You'll need to start this recipe 24 hours ahead.

4 LB SKINLESS, BONELESS CHICKEN
   THIGHS
3 TBSP SAKE
½ CUP SOY SAUCE
5–6 CLOVES GARLIC, GRATED
1 (3-INCH) KNOB FRESH GINGER,
   PEELED AND GRATED (ABOUT
   4 TBSP)
½ TSP SALT
½ TSP FRESHLY GROUND
   WHITE PEPPER

¼ CUP SESAME OIL
VEGETABLE OIL FOR FRYING
2 LARGE EGGS
2 CUPS POTATO STARCH

Serves 6–8
Gluten-free (if made with gluten-free soy sauce)

1 Cut the chicken into 3-inch pieces. In a large bowl, combine the sake, soy sauce, garlic, ginger, salt, pepper, and sesame oil. Add the chicken, stir to combine, cover with plastic wrap, and marinate overnight in the refrigerator.

2 Remove the chicken from the fridge at least 30 minutes before you plan to fry it, so the meat isn't too cold when it hits the frying oil.

3 Fill a deep-fat fryer or deep frying pan with enough vegetable oil so that the chicken pieces can be submerged completely. Heat over medium-high heat until the oil sizzles instantly upon contact with a drop of water. Once the oil is hot, break the eggs into the marinating chicken and combine by hand, making sure the egg is evenly distributed.

4 Dredge chicken pieces in batches in the potato starch.

5 Fry the chicken in batches (don't crowd the pan with chicken) until cooked through and the outer coating is crisp and gold in some areas, snowy white and crisp in others, 6–9 minutes, depending on the size of the pieces. Adjust the heat and cooking time as necessary.

6 Remove the chicken from the oil with a slotted spoon or tongs, drain on paper towels, and serve immediately. Or serve chilled, at a picnic the following day.

GEORGE AND EIKO VOJKOVICH

Skagit River Ranch

As anyone who's ever visited Skagit River Ranch in Sedro Woolley knows, George Vojkovich gives the most entertaining farm tours in the state. It helps that he's a talented talker—there never was such a man for providing a sound bite as George—but it's even more important that he really knows what he's talking about when it comes to his polyculture ranching practices.

Cattle, pigs, chickens, and turkeys share a gorgeous patch of land along the Skagit River; the riverbanks are protected by a wide swath of trees and pathways. You can see salmon swimming along to spawn in the summer, and when the spring and fall floods happen—as they do to some degree pretty much every year—George looks at it as a net positive. Except in the case of a catastrophic level of water, they've got enough high ground to keep the animals safe, and the receding waters leave behind important deposits of trace minerals that help his pastures stay nutritious.

The animal processing takes place right on the farm. George has a few gory but fascinating stories about the details, including a comparison between his cattle and a couple of conventionally raised steer that were brought in for slaughter by the USDA to evaluate the safety and capabilities of the ranch's mobile processing unit. To summarize a moderately gruesome tale: the unusable parts of Skagit River Ranch beef will compost cleanly, but this is decidedly not the case for the unusable bits of the USDA cattle.

A couple summers ago, when George and his wife, Eiko, opened their farm to guests for a tour, burger contest, and chef-farmer panel discus-

sion, someone in the audience asked the panel to define what "sustainability" meant. George was the first to speak up, and he said, "Fundamentally, it's 'do all the checks clear at the end of the month?' 'Cause if they don't, it's not sustainable, no matter what practices you're using." This is partly where Eiko comes in—George's quieter counterpart has an MBA, without which, she has said, she wouldn't be able to effectively run the farm. George handles the science (and politics), but Eiko focuses on the bottom line. She's also a lovely and efficient presence at the University District Farmers' Market on Saturday mornings. She can always spare a moment to talk recipes or weather or meticulously record your order for an upcoming holiday. And when it's time to load the truck with frozen chickens and get them to a restaurant, she moves faster than anyone. If Eiko ever decides to run for office, she'd be unbeatable.

George and Eiko's daughter, Nicole, is a regular weekend market presence these days—all stores should be so lucky to have such knowledgeable weekend help—and you might spot her gracefully riding her horse when you visit the farm. George and Eiko used to say that they'd sell only meat that they'd be willing to feed their family, by which they meant that they weren't about to let Nicole eat junk food, whether it came in a colorful plastic wrapper or on a pressed-foam meat tray. In a larger sense, it's more like the Vojkovichs have expanded their idea of family to include all the residents of Puget Sound. They don't want any of us eating such food, and they do what it takes to give us amazing alternatives.

TAVERN LAW FRIED CHICKEN

Adapted from Brian McCracken and Dana Tough, Tavern Law

The Tavern Law kitchen officially cooks their delicious chicken *sous vide* before finishing it in the fryer. While we applaud their attention to perfection, we think the simplicity of a juicy brined bird and a crisp buttermilk coating tastes just fine fried the old-fashioned way. Call us lazy. Or perhaps just realistic. Poussins are young frying chickens and, while more expensive than game hens per pound, are becoming easier to find from local farms. Aside from farmers' markets, you can also pick them up from University Seafood & Poultry or Don and Joe's at Pike Place Market. In the summertime, this chicken is great with Salty Green Potato Salad (page 48); in the winter, we opt for Blasted Broccoli (page 35) and mashed potatoes. *Note:* This recipe requires 12–24 hours of brining time.

Edible Tip

For the cleanest frying oil around, look for either rice bran oil or expeller-pressed safflower oil. Both have extremely high smoking points.

FOR THE BRINE:
3½ OZ (¾ CUPS) SALT
2 (1½ LB) POUSSINS OR GAME HENS

FOR THE CHICKEN:
1 QT VEGETABLE OR PEANUT OIL
    FOR FRYING

2 CUPS ALL-PURPOSE FLOUR
2 CUPS BUTTERMILK
SALT
FRESHLY GROUND BLACK PEPPER

Serves 4

1 In a large bowl, dissolve the salt in 2 quarts water; then add the poussins. Brine in the refrigerator for 12–24 hours.

2 Rinse the birds and cut them into quarters: breasts, and thighs with leg attached. Pull all the bones from the rib cage and remove any backbone, leaving the 2 leg quarters bone-in.

3 Heat the oil to 350°F over medium-high heat in a cast-iron Dutch oven. Dredge the quarters in flour, then dip in the buttermilk, then dredge in the flour again, and sprinkle with salt and pepper to taste. Fry the pieces (without crowding them in the pan) until golden brown and the internal temperature has reached 160°F on an instant-read thermometer inserted in the center of the breast or at the joint of a thigh quarter. Drain the chicken on a wire rack set over a baking sheet.

CHICKEN BREASTS WITH ROASTED RED PEPPERS, HEDGEHOG MUSHROOMS, AND TRUFFLED CHEESE

From Alex Corcoran

The basic idea of stuffed chicken breasts isn't a new one—in fact, Alex has made so many variations of this over the years that he once took up the challenge to literally cook it blindfolded. (Which we can't, for hopefully obvious reasons, recommend you try at home.) The inclusion of Mt. Townsend Trufflestack, an award-winning, truffle-laden version of their delicious soft-ripened Seastack cheese, is inspired. The truffle fragrance thumps quietly as a bass note in every bite. Hedgehogs are similar in flavor to chanterelles and can be found in early fall at the Foraged & Found stand at farmers' markets. Other seasonal mushrooms can be substituted, although matsutakes aren't recommended, as they don't go very well with the cheese. Depending on the time of year you're serving this dish, it goes nicely with Garlicky Greens (page 33), Blasted Spring Vegetable Salad (page 39), or Browned Braised Baby Turnips (page 54).

Edible Wine Pairing

2009 FORGERON CHARDONNAY, COLUMBIA VALLEY, $25

Forgeron winemaker Marie-Eve Gilla trained in France's Burgundy region, famous for its world-class Chardonnays. Gilla brings her Burgundy bias to Walla Walla, where she crafts this Burgundian (Chablis-like) Chardonnay, the antithesis to the oaky and buttery Chardonnays that have defined the American market.

FOR THE ROASTED RED PEPPERS:
2 RED BELL PEPPERS
2 CLOVES GARLIC
2 TBSP EXTRA-VIRGIN OLIVE OIL
SALT
FRESHLY GROUND BLACK PEPPER

FOR THE STUFFED CHICKEN BREASTS:
4 SKINLESS, BONELESS CHICKEN BREASTS

¾ STICK (6 TBSP) UNSALTED BUTTER
¼ LB HEDGEHOG MUSHROOMS
3–4 OZ TRUFFLED COW'S MILK CHEESE
SALT
FRESHLY GROUND BLACK PEPPER
¾ CUP ALL-PURPOSE FLOUR
2 TBSP OLIVE OIL

Serves 4

1 Move the top oven rack so it's about 5 inches from the broiler element. Preheat the broiler and line a baking sheet with aluminum foil. Place the whole peppers on the sheet and broil, turning them every few minutes, until their skins are entirely charred. Transfer to a bowl large enough to hold them, and cover the bowl with the foil. Allow the peppers to rest for 20 minutes.

2 Uncover the bowl and use a paring knife to remove the skins, stems, and seeds, while capturing the juice and flesh in the bowl. Cut or tear the peppers into 1-inch-wide strips. Using the flat side of a large knife, crush the garlic cloves and remove the skins. Add the garlic, olive oil, and salt and pepper to taste and allow the roasted peppers to marinate at room temperature for 2 hours, stirring occasionally.

3 Preheat the oven to 350°F. If the chicken breasts are large, insert a knife with a 1-inch blade into the center from the end of the breast, creating a pocket. Be careful not to pierce the outside. If the breasts are small, butterfly them out flat, cover with plastic wrap, and pound flat.

4 Melt 2 tablespoons of the butter in a small sauté pan and briefly cook the mushrooms until they're soft, 3–4 minutes. Fill the pocket of each chicken breast with a strip of pepper, then some of the mushroom, then the cheese, and repeat until it can hold no more. Close the opening with a toothpick, season to taste with salt and pepper, and dredge in the flour.

5 Melt the remaining 4 tablespoons butter in a large ovenproof sauté pan, add the olive oil, and cook the breasts, turning until lightly browned.

6 Transfer the pan to the oven and bake the chicken until cooked through, about 20 minutes. Serve immediately.

EDIBLE SEATTLE: THE COOKBOOK

70

GNOCCHI WITH ARTICHOKE SAUCE

From Sabrina Tinsley,
Osteria La Spiga

While there's nothing exactly wrong about a plain boiled artichoke, there's a whole lot that's exactly right about a lemony, herby delicate artichoke sauce served over tender homemade gnocchi. Artichokes are a market staple from midsummer through October, and Sabrina's sauce is the ideal midpoint between a light, summery meal and a rich pre-hibernation fall supper. When you're buying artichokes, you'll see a big size range, anywhere from egg-size baby artichokes to massive, prickly softballs. Chances are that they're all the same variety, and possibly even from the same plant. The biggest ones grow at the top of the main stalk, the babies sprout up from the base, and the medium ones are from anywhere in between but typically on the smaller side stalks. This sauce is geared for medium or large artichokes.

FOR THE GNOCCHI:

2 LB RUSSET POTATOES, PEELED
 AND COOKED IN SALTED WATER
 TO COVER UNTIL TENDER
PINCH OF SALT
1 LARGE EGG
1½ CUPS ALL-PURPOSE FLOUR, PLUS
 MORE FOR DUSTING
½ CUP SEMOLINA

FOR THE ARTICHOKE SAUCE:

4 MEDIUM-SIZE ARTICHOKES
JUICE FROM 1 LEMON
3 TBSP EXTRA-VIRGIN OLIVE OIL
1 MEDIUM ONION, CUT INTO FINE
 DICE
2 CLOVES GARLIC
LEAVES FROM 1 BUNCH FRESH
 FLAT-LEAF PARSLEY, MINCED
SALT
FRESHLY GROUND BLACK PEPPER
2 CUPS VEGETABLE STOCK
1 CUP HEAVY CREAM

Serves 4
Vegetarian

Make the gnocchi:

1 Process the hot potatoes through a ricer, directly onto your work area. Allow to cool for 15 minutes. Sprinkle the salt over the top of the riced potatoes. Using your fingers, blend in the egg, then the flour and semolina. Knead the dough into a soft, workable consistency. Add a touch more flour if the dough seems too sticky.

2 Line a baking sheet with wax paper. Using your hands, work the dough into several long cylinders about ½ inch in diameter. Dust the cylinders with flour as needed to keep them rolling smoothly, keeping in mind that too much flour will hinder you from rolling them out effectively. With a sharp knife, cut the cylinders into ½-inch pieces.

3 Once you have cut all the gnocchi, using your thumb or index and middle finger together, press down on each piece as you roll it toward yourself, curling it up around your fingers. After curling each one, dust lightly with flour and set on the lined baking sheet. Keep the gnocchi separate from each other to prevent clumping and sticking. Cover the sheet with a kitchen towel or plastic wrap while you make the sauce.

Make the artichoke sauce:

4 Prepare the artichokes by peeling away the outer leaves until you reach the tender yellow ones beneath. Cut off the spiny tip of each leaf, peel away the dark green layer from the base and stem with a paring knife or peeler, and slice off the stem, cutting it into ½-inch pieces. Next, quarter the heart lengthwise and remove the choke with a spoon. Slice the heart in half again (the heart should be divided into eighths lengthwise) and plunge the pieces into a large bowl of cold water mixed with the lemon juice.

5 In a medium saucepan over medium-high heat, heat the olive oil. Add the onion and garlic and sauté until tender, 5–8 minutes, making sure to reduce the heat if necessary to avoid browning. Add the parsley (reserve about 1 tablespoon for garnish) and sauté 2–3 minutes on high. Drain the artichoke pieces, add to the pan, and season to taste with salt and pepper. Sauté for several minutes. Add the stock just so it comes below the level of the artichokes, cover the pan, and simmer until the artichokes are completely tender, about 5 minutes.

6 When the artichokes are tender, carefully transfer the mixture to a food processor or blender and process until a few chunks remain but the mixture is fairly smooth. Return the puree to the pan. Add the cream and heat through the sauce over low heat. Check the seasoning.

Finish the dish:

7 Bring several quarts of water to a boil in a large stockpot. Add half the gnocchi to the boiling water. Do not stir. When the gnocchi rise to the surface, let cook for about 2 more minutes, strain, and transfer to a large warm serving bowl. Add the remaining gnocchi to the boiling water and, while they cook, dress the first batch with one-third of the hot artichoke sauce. Toss carefully with a broad silicone spatula, being careful not to break the gnocchi. Strain the second batch of gnocchi, place on top of the first batch, and repeat with half the remaining sauce.

8 Offer the remaining sauce on the side, adding more to the individual bowls when the gnocchi is served. Garnish with the reserved parsley and pass Parmigiano-Reggiano around the table.

BOEUF BOURGUIGNON

*From Thierry Rautureau,
Chef in the Hat, Luc*

Thierry's version of boeuf bourguignon is a straight-up classic: sheer beefy perfection, it is utterly worth every dirty pot and cholesterol point. Thierry says it reminds him of his childhood in Nantes. We should all be so lucky to eat this well as children. When shopping for beef, you won't find a cut labeled "beef shoulder"—what you want is either a chuck roast of some sort or, from a bit lower on the shoulder, a cut labeled either "arm roast" or "round bone roast." The latter options are incredible for all recipes where the beef needs to cook low and slow. The texture never gets mushy, and the flavor is as rich as can be. Chuck cuts are widely available, but check Olsen Farms or Skagit River Ranch at the farmers' markets for the round bone/arm cuts. *Note:* This recipe needs to marinate overnight.

Edible Tip

In an effort to inspire a classic Gallic shrug from Thierry, we suggest a New World counterpart to one of France's Burgundies for the wine in this stew. Syncline's Pinot Noir has the depth and richness needed, or opt for their spicy 2009 Grenache-Carignan blend.

2 LB BEEF SHOULDER, CUT INTO 2-INCH PIECES
1 ONION, CUT INTO LARGE DICE
2 CARROTS, CUT INTO LARGE DICE
2 STALKS CELERY, CUT INTO LARGE DICE
2 DRIED BAY LEAVES
4 SPRIGS FRESH THYME
7 SPRIGS FRESH FLAT-LEAF PARSLEY
¼ TSP BLACK PEPPERCORNS
1 (750 ML) BOTTLE RED WINE, PREFERABLY A BIG-FLAVORED ONE FROM WASHINGTON STATE
SALT
FRESHLY GROUND BLACK PEPPER

1 TBSP CANOLA OIL
¼ LB SLAB BACON, CUT INTO LARGE DICE
½ STICK (4 TBSP) UNSALTED BUTTER
¼ CUP ALL-PURPOSE FLOUR
4 CUPS BEEF STOCK
2 LARGE YUKON GOLD POTATOES, PEELED AND CUT INTO LARGE DICE
1 LB PEARL ONIONS, BLANCHED AND PEELED
1 LB BUTTON MUSHROOMS, DICED

Serves 6 generously

1 Put the beef chunks in a large bowl and add the onion, carrots, and celery. In a piece of cheesecloth, tie together a bouquet garni of the bay leaves, thyme, parsley, and peppercorns and add to the bowl. Pour in the bottle of wine. Cover and let marinate in the refrigerator overnight, stirring the mixture once or twice over the course of the evening.

2 The next day, remove the meat from the marinade and dry the pieces in a shallow pan lined with several layers of paper towels. Remove the vegetables and reserve them separately, along with the bouquet garni. Reserve the wine. Season the beef with salt and pepper.

3 In a large Dutch oven over medium heat, warm the canola oil. Add the bacon and cook until browned and the fat is rendered, about 5 minutes. Remove the bacon from the pot and set aside. In single-layer batches, brown the beef chunks on all sides, then set aside. Brown the reserved onion, carrots, and celery, about 10 minutes. Add additional canola oil to the pot if there is not enough bacon fat to brown all of the beef and vegetables.

4 Return the beef to the pot with the vegetables and add 3 tablespoons of the butter. Sprinkle with the flour and cook, stirring, for about 3 minutes. Add the reserved wine and deglaze the pot, scraping up all the browned bits from the bottom. Add the bacon and stock and bring to a boil. Skim off the scum that rises to the top; once the scum is removed, add the bouquet garni. Simmer, covered, over medium-low heat until the beef is very tender, about 1½ hours. Remove the bouquet garni.

5 Toward the end of the beef's cooking time, bring the potatoes to a boil in a separate saucepan covered generously with salted water. Cook until tender, about 15 minutes.

6 In a medium sauté pan, melt 3 tablespoons of the butter over medium-high heat. Add the pearl onions and sauté for 3–4 minutes. Add the mushrooms to the onions and cook until both onions and mushrooms are golden brown, about 5 minutes longer. Season to taste with salt and pepper.

7 Serve the stew in bowls, garnished with the pearl onions, mushrooms, and potatoes.

MUSHROOM STROGANOFF

This vegetarian meal is total comfort food. Served over buttered noodles or rice or with toasted bread, it comes together in just a few minutes and reheats well, too. While grocery store crimini mushrooms work fine with this dish, it becomes an utter luxury if your favorite wild mushroom is in season—and since around here you can find wild mushrooms most of the year, it's fun to experiment. Chanterelles, porcini, and morels are all delicious, and this is a nice way of stretching their flavor if you have only a handful of these expensive treats. Another option is Cascadia Mushrooms, a Bellingham-area farm that raises shiitake, Wine Cap, Lion's Mane, and Turkey Tail mushrooms and sells them at the University District Farmers' Market. For a wider range of straight-from-the-forest varieties, check the Foraged & Found stand at the same market.

Edible Tip

Whole-milk quark from Appel Farms is a thick cultured cheese with a milder flavor than sour cream. It's fairly easy to find in the dairy case of Washington's grocery stores—typically near the sour cream tubs. Crème fraîche, Greek-style plain whole-milk yogurt, or sour cream can be substituted for the quark, but each will add a different degree of tanginess to the dish. We like quark or crème fraîche the best because they're the least tangy.

5⅓ TBSP UNSALTED BUTTER
1 MEDIUM YELLOW ONION, COARSELY CHOPPED
1½ LB ASSORTED MUSHROOMS, WIPED CLEAN AS NECESSARY AND COARSELY CHOPPED (BOTH CAPS AND STEMS)
GENEROUS GRATINGS OF FRESH NUTMEG
1 CUP WHOLE-MILK QUARK, AT ROOM TEMPERATURE
SALT
FRESHLY GROUND BLACK PEPPER

Serves 4
Vegetarian
Gluten-free (if served with rice)

1 Melt the butter in a medium sauté pan over medium heat. Add the onion and cook, stirring, until the edges of the onion are light brown and the centers are transparent and pale yellow. Reduce the heat to medium-low.

2 Add the mushrooms and cook, covered but stirring occasionally, until tender. Grate the nutmeg over the mushrooms to taste. Reduce the heat to low and stir in the quark until smooth. Season to taste with salt and pepper. Serve immediately with the starch of your choice.

SOUTH INDIAN CHANA MASALA SOUP

Adapted from Chili's Restaurant

Across the street from the University District Farmers' Market sits a funky block of tiny mom-n-pop restaurants. Within a few yards, a diner can find inexpensive North Indian, Filipino, Hawaiian, Chinese, Japanese, South Indian, Egyptian, and Trinidadian meals. While tasty things can be found at each establishment, the South Indian fare of *dosas*, *poori*, *sambar*, and *chana masala* at Chili's is our favorite. In part, this is because it's nearly impossible to find South Indian elsewhere in the Seattle area, and once you develop a *dosa* habit, it's hard to quit. In part, it's the proprietor (her childhood nickname was "Chili," like the fiery pepper, thanks to a slight inclination for back-talking her mama), a lovely, generous woman who's fun to visit with. Finally, the *chana masala* that comes with puffy golden brown *pooris* are some of the greatest chickpeas on the planet. Our version is good, but not magical. We leave the magic to Chili's. *Note:* The chickpeas need to soak overnight.

2 CUPS DRIED ALVAREZ FARM
　CHICKPEAS
1 TSP BLACK TEA LEAVES
　OR 2 BLACK TEA BAGS
½ CUP GHEE, OR ½ STICK (4 TBSP)
　UNSALTED BUTTER PLUS
　¼ CUP PEANUT OIL
1 MEDIUM ONION, DICED
6–12 DRIED OR 2–3 FRESH
　CURRY LEAVES
2 TSP BROWN MUSTARD SEEDS
1 TBSP WORLD SPICE SOUTH
　INDIAN MADRAS CURRY BLEND

1 CUP FINELY CHOPPED FRESH OR
　(DRAINED) CANNED TOMATOES
7 CUPS VEGETABLE STOCK
　OR WATER
⅛ TSP CAYENNE PEPPER,
　OR TO TASTE (OPTIONAL)
KOSHER SALT

Serves 4
Vegetarian
Gluten-free

1 Soak the chickpeas in generous water to cover overnight. The next day, drain and rinse the chickpeas; then pour them into a medium Dutch oven and add the tea leaves (placed in a metal tea ball). Cover the chickpeas entirely with water, plus 2 inches. Bring to a boil over high heat, and then cover the pot and lower the heat to keep them at a moderate simmer until they are close to fully cooked—tender but not quite perfect, 60–75 minutes. Drain and set aside.

2 In a large, deep sauté pan, heat the ghee or the butter and peanut oil over high heat. Add the onion, curry leaves, mustard seeds, and curry powder and fry, stirring constantly, for 1 minute. Lower the heat to medium and continue to cook and stir for about 5 more minutes. Stir in the tomatoes and cook, stirring only occasionally, for another 5 minutes. Fold in the chickpeas and add the stock. Season to taste with cayenne pepper and salt. Simmer until the chickpeas are done exactly to your liking, another 20–30 minutes. Serve ladled into soup bowls.

Edible Tips

We specifically call out Alvarez Farm chickpeas for an important reason: they are likely a few months to a year old and cook as they should.

　For different kinds of *chana*-friendly curry powders to replace the Madras blend or to hunt down black mustard seeds to substitute for the brown variety, check out local Indian groceries. Our favorites are Continental Spices (7819 Aurora N, Seattle) and Pabla Indian Cuisine Sweets & Spices (364 Renton Center Way SW, Renton).

MAIN DISHES

SAAG PANEER

Okay, so Indian spices aren't grown in Western Washington—but thanks to an abundance of local spinach and the tasty paneer made by Ferndale's Appel Farms, we can still claim this classic Indian dish as local. Appel Farms' version is better than the house-made cheese served at any number of local restaurants; it has a toothsome texture and mild sweetness that gives a noticeable contrast to the rich, savory spinach. For a spicier kick, substitute mustard greens for a portion of the spinach; you'll commonly find them sold in small bunches at Asian flower stands or on farm tables where the farmer happens to appreciate spicy greens. Mustard greens offer a wasabi-style heat—they clear your sinuses instead of burning your lips.

If you don't have clarified butter (ghee) on hand, just use a half-and-half blend of butter and canola or peanut oil. Be sure to serve this with basmati rice and grilled naan or pita.

Edible Tip

The best spices are recently purchased and freshly ground; the older your spices, the more likely the final dish will tasty muddy. World Spice, on the Hill Climb below Pike Place Market, has everything you need for this dish, and they can grind all the spices for you.

1 LB FRESH SPINACH
½ TSP SALT
¾ TSP GARAM MASALA
½ TSP GROUND CORIANDER
¼ TSP TURMERIC
¼ TSP GROUND CUMIN
¼ CUP GHEE
1 MEDIUM ONION, MINCED
2 TBSP PEELED AND MINCED FRESH GINGER

¼ CUP HEAVY CREAM OR EVAPORATED MILK
¾ LB APPEL FARMS PANEER, CUT INTO 2-INCH CUBES

Serves 4
Vegetarian
Gluten-free

1 In a food processor, alternate adding handfuls of spinach and tablespoons of water, up to ¾ cup water, blending between additions. When you have a wet, smooth puree, whirl in the salt.

2 In a small dish, combine the garam masala, coriander, turmeric, and cumin.

3 Set a large, heavy skillet over medium-high heat and add the ghee. Once it is thoroughly hot, add the onion and ginger. Stir constantly, frying until the onion is soft and medium brown. Pour in the spice mixture all at once and stir until the spices are slightly fried and completely coating the onion. Slowly pour in the spinach puree, stirring to blend with the spiced onion. Reduce the heat to medium-low and simmer, uncovered, until most of the water has evaporated, about 15 minutes.

4 Stir in the cream, add the paneer, and cover. Cook for about 5 minutes, until the paneer is warmed through. Adjust the seasonings to taste and serve hot.

MARINATED TOFU STEAK

From Cheeky Café

When a plate of tofu has several dedicated meat lovers fighting over the scraps, you know it's great. Originally, we were sure that Cheeky Café—tucked into the edge of the Central District—was taking advantage of one of the nearby tofu producers. Not so; they say it's really all about letting it drain overnight and giving the tofu steaks a quick sear on each side. Each slab gets a crispy, nicely seasoned exterior that contains a lovely custard-like interior. If you can, swing over to Northwest Tofu (Nineteenth and Jackson) or Than Son Tofu (Twelfth and Yesler) to pick up the freshest possible product. Uwajimaya is another fine place for quality tofu—or you can find Island Spring tofu from Vashon Island at just about every local co-op and grocery store. While Cheeky Café uses the medium (midpoint between silken and firm tofu densities), opt for firm if medium isn't available.

1¼ LB MEDIUM TOFU

1 CLOVE GARLIC, MINCED, PLUS 2 TBSP MINCED GARLIC

1 SMALL NUB FRESH GINGER, PEELED AND GRATED

2 TBSP VEGETABLE OIL

½ LB BUTTON MUSHROOMS, THINLY SLICED

½ CUP PLUS 1 TBSP SOY SAUCE

½ CUP PLUS 1 TBSP MIRIN

⅓ CUP ALL-PURPOSE FLOUR

¼ LB FRESH SPINACH, HEAVY STEMS REMOVED

Serves 4
Vegan

1 Divide the tofu into 5-ounce squares or rectangular portions. Place a wire rack in a baking pan, and set the tofu squares on the rack. Pat the 1 clove minced garlic and the ginger on one side of each tofu steak. Set the pan in the fridge and let the tofu drain overnight.

2 About 30 minutes before you're ready to eat, warm the vegetable oil in a medium saucepan over medium-high heat. Sauté the mushrooms and remaining 2 tablespoons minced garlic in the oil until just tender. Turn off heat. Combine the soy sauce and mirin and add to the mushrooms. Set aside.

3 Heat a large nonstick frying pan to medium heat. (*Note:* dry nonstick pans should not be heated beyond medium heat.) Dredge both sides of the drained tofu steaks in the flour. Fry the tofu steaks, ginger/garlic side up, for a few minutes, until the bottom is golden brown. Flip each steak. When the second side is golden brown, pour the mushroom sauce over the tofu steaks and cook until the sauce thickens and coats the tofu. Turn off the heat.

4 Divide the spinach evenly among 4 shallow bowls or dinner plates. Place a tofu steak on top of the spinach, and pour excess sauce on the tofu and around the spinach.

Edible Wine Pairing

2010 EFESTE EVERGREEN RIESLING, EVERGREEN VINEYARD, COLUMBIA VALLEY, $16

This Riesling begs for Asian spices. The cool climate of the Evergreen Vineyard at 1,300 feet elevation, further cooled by the neighboring Columbia River, helps retain high acidity and low alcohol, making it a food-friendly wine. Apricot, green tea, and minerals make this a complex off-dry Riesling.

SPRING PEA AND LEMON CREAM PASTA

From Salish Lodge

We are profoundly in favor of fresh vegetables, particularly in early June, when our slow spring finally arrives in edible form. Market tables become riotously colorful, flavors are bright and sweet, and a quick sauté is all that's necessary to turn these great raw ingredients into a decadent meal. Favas are the real surprise here: they look like lima beans but taste more like an English pea. Depending on the weather, they'll make an appearance right after Mother's Day and can stick around through September. You want fat, fresh, bright green beans for this recipe; if you can't find them, substitute more peas or carrots. The lemony cream that binds these vegetables together is shamefully rich, and we wouldn't change a single calorie. If you insist, you can lighten it up by switching some of the heavy cream for half-and-half. Or keep it as is and have a small portion together with a generous salad.

Edible Tip

Valley Doe, an aged raw goat's milk cheese, has a mildly nutty flavor and lush creaminess. Imported *myzithra* would be an acceptable substitution.

4 ½ CUPS HEAVY CREAM
GRATED ZEST FROM 1 LEMON
1 SHALLOT, MINCED
1 THYME STEM
1 PARSLEY STEM
1 CLOVE GARLIC, MINCED
1 CUP FRESH ENGLISH PEAS
SALT
FRESHLY GROUND WHITE PEPPER
1 TBSP OLIVE OIL
⅓ CUP FRESH YOUNG FAVA BEANS
⅓ CUP CARROTS, CUT INTO
  SMALL PIECES
⅓ CUP FRESH SUGAR PEAS,
  BLANCHED
⅓ CUP CORN KERNELS, CUT FRESH
  FROM THE COB OR (DRAINED)
  CANNED
¾ CUP CIPOLLINI ONIONS, ROASTED
  AND PEELED
4 ½ CUPS COOKED TROFIE PASTA
¾ CUP SHAVED VALLEY DOE CHEESE
  FROM RIVER VALLEY RANCH

Serves 4–6

1 Combine the cream, lemon zest, shallot, thyme and parsley stems, and garlic in a large pot with plenty of extra room (to allow for the cream to boil up). Set the pot over medium-low heat and reduce by half, stirring frequently. Strain the solids out of the cream.

2 Add 1 cup of the lemon cream to a blender with the English peas and blend until smooth. Slowly whisk this mixture into the remaining lemon cream in the pot. Season to taste with salt and white pepper. Cover and remove from the heat.

3 In a large sauté pan, heat the olive oil over medium-high heat. Sauté the fava beans, carrots, fresh peas, corn, and roasted onions until all the vegetables are lightly cooked and still fairly fresh and crunchy, just a few minutes. Add the pea and lemon cream and cooked pasta to the sautéed vegetables, and heat through, stirring gently to blend. Once heated, divide the pasta among individual serving bowls and garnish with shaved Valley Doe cheese.

Edible Wine Pairing

2010 MATTHEWS ESTATE SAUVIGNON BLANC, COLUMBIA VALLEY, $20

Matthews Estate makes their Sauvignon Blanc consistently in the Sancerre style: complex and balanced in fruit and acidity. The 2010 Sauvignon Blanc was made with no oak, meaning a cleaner, fresher wine that cuts through creamy sauces. The grapefruit and grapefruit zest acidity complements the sweet flavors of this dish while neutralizing its creaminess.

RAZOR CLAM LINGUINE

Adapted from the Washington Department of Fish and Wildlife

Fresh razor clams are incredibly sweet and meaty, and relatively easy to dig yourself during their short, sporadic winter and spring seasons on the Washington coast. They're surprisingly fast, and their thin, easily shattered shells are the reason behind the rule that you have to keep the first dozen or so that you dig—but with their average length of 5 inches, one person's daily limit will be plenty to make dinner for four. Anyone over the age of fifteen needs an official license to dig, but they're easily available in all our coastal towns.

All the information about razor clam season, locations, limits, and water conditions is available from the Washington Department of Fish and Wildlife (WDFW. wa.gov). The two most important pieces of information are the dates when it's permitted to dig and the overall health of the water during a planned dig. Occasionally, scheduled digs are canceled due to bacteria in the water, when the clams could make people sick.

If you're not up for the adventure of digging the clams yourself, frozen razor clam meat is frequently available at Wild Salmon Seafood Market. A 1-pound package of frozen clam meat makes about 1½ cups chopped clams.

½ STICK (4 TBSP) UNSALTED BUTTER
¼ CUP EXTRA-VIRGIN OLIVE OIL
1 CUP FINELY CHOPPED ONIONS
2 CLOVES GARLIC, MINCED
SALT
FRESHLY GROUND BLACK PEPPER
1 CUP DRY WHITE WINE
¾ LB LINGUINE
1½ CUPS CHOPPED (½-INCH) RAZOR CLAM MEAT
1 CUP FINELY CHOPPED FRESH PARSLEY
1 TBSP CHOPPED FRESH OREGANO
RED PEPPER FLAKES (UP TO 1 TBSP)
½ CUP GRATED PARMESAN CHEESE, PLUS MORE FOR GARNISH

Serves 4

1 Bring a large pot of salted water to a boil for the pasta.

2 Heat the butter and olive oil together in a large saucepan over medium heat until the butter melts. Add the onions and garlic, season to taste with salt and black pepper, and cook until almost tender, about 5 minutes, stirring a few times. Adjust the heat to medium-low, add the wine, and simmer until the liquid reduces by about two-thirds, about 10 minutes. When you add the wine, add the pasta to the boiling water and cook according to the package instructions.

3 Add the clams, parsley, oregano, and red pepper to taste to the reduced sauce; simmer for 2–3 minutes to heat the clams through. Taste for seasoning and add more salt and black pepper if needed.

4 Drain the pasta and transfer to a large serving bowl. Add the sauce and Parmesan and toss until well mixed. Serve immediately, topped with more cheese, if desired.

Edible Tip

Once you've dug them, cleaning the clams is easy, if a little tedious. Drop them in boiling water for a few seconds until their shells pop open. Snip off the tough, skinny neck; slice them lengthwise; and cut out all the dark, digestive bits, leaving the white meat. Give them a final rinse to remove any last bits of sand, and either cook immediately or pack into plastic bags and freeze right away. They'll keep up to a year.

CORNMEAL-CRUSTED HALIBUT CHEEKS
WITH MAMA LIL'S DIPPING SAUCE

From Jess Thomson

Seattle sandwich lovers owe a great debt to Mama Lil's—these peppers have been gracing restaurant menus and our home-made sandwiches since the early nineties. More recently, what started as a sandwich topper has been turning up in more surprising places, including Jess's not-really-tartar-at-all tartar sauce. We like the sauce so much it's ruined actual tartar sauce for us. You have been warned.

For the fish itself, halibut cheeks are just as irreplaceable as the Mama Lil's. They're the easiest possible way of making fish and chips because they're already two-bite-size and there's no skin. Best of all is the texture—it's all long, thin shreds, like pulled pork or a round bone roast. Cheeks are also cheaper than halibut fillets, a decided bonus when feeding four people. They're regularly found at both Wild Salmon Seafood and Pike Place Fish Market (see Resources, page 162).

FOR MAMA LIL'S DIPPING SAUCE:

1 CUP MAYONNAISE
¼ CUP FINELY CHOPPED YELLOW
   ONION
¼ CUP MAMA LIL'S PEPPERS (WITH
   OIL), FINELY CHOPPED
JUICE OF ½ LEMON

FOR THE CORNMEAL-CRUSTED
HALIBUT CHEEKS:
CANOLA OIL FOR DEEP FRYING

½ CUP ALL-PURPOSE FLOUR
3 LARGE EGGS, BEATEN
2 CUPS MEDIUM-GROUND
   CORNMEAL
SALT
FRESHLY GROUND BLACK PEPPER
1 LB HALIBUT CHEEKS (4 LARGE
   OR 8 SMALL), PATTED DRY

Serves 4
Dairy-free

Make the sauce:

1 Mix the mayonnaise, onion, peppers, and lemon juice in a small bowl to blend. Set aside.

Prepare and cook the halibut:

2 Fill a large, heavy skillet with canola oil to a depth of about ½ inch. Heat the oil to 350°F over medium-high heat.

3 While the oil heats, place the flour, eggs, and cornmeal each in a separate wide, shallow bowl (or on 3 separate plates). Season each with salt and pepper, and stir each with a fork to blend. Dip each halibut cheek first in the flour, then in the eggs, then in the cornmeal, making sure to coat the fish on both sides each time.

4 When the oil is hot, fry the fish a few pieces at a time until golden brown, about 2 minutes per side. Drain the fish briefly on a paper towel–lined plate.

5 Serve the halibut cheeks immediately with the dipping sauce.

ROASTED WILD ALASKAN BLACK COD WITH KOMBU DASHI, KALE, AND SAGE

From Jason Wilson, Crush

Considering just how far away Alaska really is, it's a little odd that we consider wild Alaska fish "local." But when you consider how many fishing boats are based in Western Washington, and how much of the country is eating farmed fish that ships to them from even farther away than Alaska—not to mention that many of the fish populations migrate past us during their lives—well, we forgive ourselves.

We work to encourage the idea of "nose-to-tail" seafood, and broth is a great beginner step in that process. Fish stock is simple and cheap to make, and it'll blow your mind with its oceanic fragrance. Fishmongers can supply you with the meaty scraps you need. Layered in a bowl with black cod (also called sablefish; it's a "best choice" on the Monterey Bay Aquarium Seafood Watch card) and shreds of kale, this winter soup cures whatever might be ailing you—and leaves guests clamoring for the recipe.

Edible Tip

Kombu is the broad, flat, dried kelp that's easy to find in Asian markets. If you buy a seaweed license from the state, you can harvest your own fresh kelp. The Washington Department of Fish and Wildlife issues the licenses and provides information about marine closures from bacteria. Visit their website (WDFW.wa.gov) for more information.

1 TBSP PLUS 2 TSP KOSHER SALT
5 DRIED PORCINI MUSHROOMS
2 TBSP EXTRA-VIRGIN OLIVE OIL
1 YELLOW ONION, THINLY SLICED
2 CLOVES GARLIC, SMASHED
2 INCHES PEELED FRESH GINGER, THINLY SLICED
1 STALK CELERY, THINLY SLICED
2 BAY LEAVES
3 LB FISH BONES AND SCRAPS
4 SHEETS DRY KOMBU OR 1 LB FRESH PACIFIC KELP
½ CUP DRY WHITE WINE

4 (6 OZ) WILD ALASKAN BLACK COD FILLETS
2 TBSP BUTTER
1 TBSP FINELY CHOPPED SHALLOTS
1 LEEK, ROUGHLY CHOPPED
1 TSP KOSHER SALT
1 CUP STEMMED, THINLY SLICED KALE
1 TBSP CHOPPED FRESH SAGE

Serves 4
Gluten-free

1 In a spice or coffee grinder, grind 1 tablespoon of the salt and the porcini mushrooms together until very fine (roughly 1 minute); then sift the mixture through a fine-mesh sieve. Cover and set aside.

2 Heat the olive oil in a large soup pot over medium-high heat. Add the onion, garlic, ginger, celery, bay leaves, and 1 teaspoon salt and cook until the vegetables are fragrant and sweating, about 5 minutes. Add the fish bones and scraps, kombu, and wine and simmer for 10 minutes. Add 3 quarts water and simmer slowly over medium heat for 1¼ hours, skimming off any impurities, gray matter, and excess ingredients that float to the surface of the broth. Strain the broth through a fine-mesh strainer, discard the solids, and simmer the broth again for 15 minutes. Remove from the heat and keep warm.

3 Preheat the oven to 185°F. Line a sheet pan with parchment paper. Place the cod fillets on the pan and season liberally with the porcini salt. Place the pan in the oven for 38 minutes.

4 While the fish is baking, place a sauté pan over medium heat and add the butter, shallots, leek, and remaining 1 teaspoon salt. Sauté until tender but not browned. If the vegetables start to brown, add a couple of tablespoons of the broth. When the leek is tender, add the kale and sage and sauté until the kale is soft.

5 Divide the kale among 4 serving bowls. Using a spatula, place the black cod on the kale, pour the broth on and around the fish, and serve.

2009 SYNCLINE GRÜNER VELTLINER, UNDERWOOD MOUNTAIN VINEYARD, COLUMBIA GORGE, $20

The 2009 Syncline Grüner Veltliner, made exclusively with fruit from the Underwood Mountain Vineyard, distinctive for its steep hills in the Columbia Gorge, was made for a fatty fish dish with delicate umami flavors like this one. The acidity in this Grüner Veltliner neutralizes the fatty fish, while the saline qualities complement the umami of the kombu dashi.

XINH'S MEDITERRANEAN MUSSELS IN CURRY SAUCE

From Xinh Dwelley,
Xinh's Clam and Oyster House

Xinh has a way with shellfish, and this rich curry manages to comfort and surprise at the same time. Her mussels are sourced from Taylor Shellfish—she worked there before opening her restaurant in Shelton, right on the Totten Inlet—and now her seafood house has gained renown for her preparations, which all start with some of the world's best bivalves. Pick a curry powder of your choice, but before you grab one from the grocery store, we suggest stopping by World Spice, on the area known as Hill Climb across from Pike Place Market. They have approximately umpteen house-blended curries made with whole spices and will grind them for you. Few places on earth smell as nice as their jars of curry.

5 LB MUSSELS, SCRUBBED CLEAN (DISCARD ANY MUSSELS WITH BROKEN SHELLS OR THAT WON'T CLOSE)

½ STICK (4 TBSP) UNSALTED BUTTER

1 TSP MINCED GARLIC

¾ CUP CHOPPED ONION

1 CUP COCONUT MILK

1 TBSP CURRY POWDER

1½ TBSP SOY SAUCE

½ TSP SUGAR

½ CUP UNSALTED DRY-ROASTED PEANUTS

SALT

FRESHLY GROUND BLACK PEPPER

CAYENNE PEPPER (OPTIONAL)

CHOPPED SCALLION FOR GARNISH

CHOPPED FRESH CILANTRO FOR GARNISH

HOT STEAMED RICE OR RICE NOODLES FOR SERVING

Serves 4 generously

1 Bring 3 cups water to a boil in a stockpot over high heat. Add the mussels, cover, and steam until they have all opened. Drain and remove the meat from the shells. Discard any mussels that won't open.

2 In a large saucepan over medium-high heat, melt the butter. Add the garlic and onion, and sauté until the onion is translucent. Lower the heat to medium. Add the coconut milk, curry powder, soy sauce, sugar, and peanuts, mixing well after each addition. Season with salt, black pepper, and cayenne to taste. Gently stir in the mussel meat. Raise the heat and bring to a brief boil to warm up the mussels.

3 Sprinkle the mussels with the scallion and cilantro just before serving. Serve hot over rice or noodles.

PAN-SEARED CAPE CLEARE COHO SALMON
WITH MARINATED FENNEL

*From Craig Hetherington,
Taste Restaurant*

In a town where restaurants and home barbecues brim over with wild salmon, it's interesting to learn people's preferences for species. Craig Hetherington loves coho—sometimes called silver—which, out at the coast, is the one sportfishermen are likely to catch. They have less oil than Kings but a slightly tangy flavor that is quite addictive. Craig buys his fish from Cape Cleare, an old-fashioned outlet that uses a hook and line to catch each salmon by hand. Their careful handling means firm, luscious, incredibly fresh-tasting salmon, which you can pick up at the Port Townsend Farmers' Market or Food Co-op, or order directly from the fisherman (see Resources, page 162).

Craig keeps this dish light, serving it with Green Lentil Salad (page 38). We suggest finishing with the Gothberg Farms Chèvre Tart (page 142) for dessert. *Note:* The fennel in this dish needs to marinate for 24 hours, so plan ahead.

1 LARGE FENNEL BULB, TRIMMED
   OF STALKS AND FRONDS
GRATED ZEST AND JUICE FROM
   2 BLOOD ORANGES
1 TBSP EXTRA-VIRGIN OLIVE OIL,
   PLUS MORE FOR SERVING

PINCH OF KOSHER SALT,
   PLUS MORE TO TASTE
20 OZ SKIN-ON CAPE CLEARE COHO
   SALMON, CUT INTO 4 FILLETS
1 TBSP CANOLA OIL

Serves 4

1 The day before serving, slice the fennel bulb against the grain very thinly, using a mandoline or other handheld slicer, and place in a small bowl. Add the orange zest and juice. Add the olive oil and salt, toss to combine, cover, and let marinate in the refrigerator overnight.

2 The next day, preheat the oven to 400°F. Season the salmon liberally with salt on the cut side. Heat the canola oil in a large ovenproof sauté pan. When the oil is hot, gently place the salmon in the pan, skin side up, using a motion that goes away from your body to avoid being splashed by the hot oil. Cook until the salmon has a crispy sear, about 2 minutes.

3 Transfer the pan to the oven and cook for another 3–5 minutes. Do not flip the fish; leave it seared side down. The internal temperature in the fattest part of the fish should register 110°F on an instant-read thermometer. Pull the pan out of the oven and let the fish rest for about 5 minutes.

4 To serve, place a salmon fillet seared side up (skin side down) on each serving plate and top with the marinated fennel. Drizzle the salmon with a little olive oil for some added flavor and color.

Edible Wine Pairing

2008 CHINOOK CABERNET FRANC, YAKIMA VALLEY, $22

Chinook makes their single-varietal Cabernet Franc in a Chinon (Loire Valley) style. Minimal processing in the vineyards as well as the winery translates to soft tannins, elegant fruit (raspberries, cherries), and redeeming acidity on the finish. It's that pleasant acidity on the long finish that neutralizes the oily salmon. What's more, the sweet licorice notes in this elegant Cabernet Franc echo the marinated fennel in the dish.

REEFNET SALMON WITH SALSA VERDE

From Seth Caswell, Emmer & Rye

Several years ago, Seth had the chance to participate in Riley Starks's "Chefs in Raingear" program on Lummi Island, where chefs get to participate in a day of reefnet salmon fishing. This technique was practiced for centuries by coastal tribes using canoes and cedar nets, but today it involves small platforms and nylon nets and relies on human spotters to watch for the schools of salmon swimming over the small submerged nets. It results in zero wasted bycatch and sweet, nonstressed salmon.

Salmon harvested this way has been included in the Slow Food U.S. Ark of Taste, a catalog of heirloom food products with a special connection to the history of a place that are in danger of extinction. You can find reefnet-caught salmon around Seattle, or join a buying club or CSA in other areas (see Resources, page 162). Served together with Seth's Salmon Run Vegetables (page 47), this preparation is a knockout plate of early summer's finest ingredients.

FOR THE SALSA VERDE:

½ CUP LIGHTLY PACKED
    FRESH BASIL LEAVES
½ CUP LIGHTLY PACKED
    FRESH PARSLEY
¼ CUP LIGHTLY PACKED
    FRESH MINT LEAVES
1 SMALL CLOVE GARLIC, MINCED
1 TSP KOSHER SALT
1½ CUPS EXTRA-VIRGIN OLIVE OIL
2 CUPS LOOSELY PACKED TORN
    FRESH-BAKED BREAD
    (WITHOUT THE CRUST)
¼ CUP WHITE VERJUICE
    OR FRESH LEMON JUICE

FOR THE SALMON:

4 (5–6 OZ) SKIN-ON REEFNET-
    CAUGHT WILD SALMON FILLETS
SALT
FRESHLY GROUND BLACK PEPPER
2 TSP OLIVE OIL
1 TSP UNSALTED BUTTER

Serves 4

Make the salsa verde:

1 Place the basil, parsley, mint, garlic, and salt in a food processor. With the machine running, add the olive oil in a slow, steady stream. Add the chunks of bread and continue to process until the bread is gravel-size. Add the verjuice or a couple of squeezes of lemon, tasting for a balance of acidity and sweetness. Set aside at room temperature. (If made the day before, refrigerate and bring to room temperature before serving.)

Cook the salmon:

2 Season both sides of the salmon fillets with salt and pepper. In a large nonstick sauté pan, heat the olive oil until almost smoking over medium-high heat. Add the butter. As the butter is browning, add the salmon, skin side down. Using a spatula, press the salmon into the pan and decrease the heat to medium-low. Let the skin crisp for 2–3 minutes; then carefully flip the fish over in the pan. Turn the heat off and let the fish cook in the residual heat for another minute or so. (You may need to increase the cooking time, depending on the thickness of your salmon.)

3 To serve, place a salmon fillet on each serving plate and spoon the salsa verde around the salmon.

SALMON TACOS

Adapted from Amy Grondin

It's common to find fish tacos that are made with fried tidbits of bland white fish—tilapia, cod, halibut—but you might as well just eat fish and chips. Amy Grondin (page 91) and her husband eat plenty of salmon tacos when they're out fishing. Obviously their fishing boat doesn't come equipped with a big outdoor grill, but we love to have that charred flavor on both the fish and the tortillas, so we've given her recipe a grilled twist. No two people seem to accessorize their tacos in the same way. One person insists on Mexican *crema*; another wants thick American sour cream. One person wants avocado slices; one would rather eat rat poison than come anywhere near an avocado. And within any family you can find a big range of chile pepper tolerance. We include the tangy, crunchy slaw because it's a basic building block of all fish tacos—but other than that, go with personal preference.

Edible Tip

If you want to make these tacos more like ones from our great local taco trucks, look for 4-inch corn tortillas, and use two of them per taco instead of one. These bite-size tortillas are most easy to find at south-end grocery stores or your neighborhood *tienda*.

FOR THE CABBAGE SLAW:
2 CUPS SHREDDED GREEN CABBAGE
⅓ CUP THINLY SLICED WALLA
    WALLA OR OTHER SWEET ONION
2 TBSP RICE VINEGAR
2 TBSP GRAPESEED OR CANOLA OIL
JUICE FROM ½ LIME
KOSHER SALT
FRESHLY GROUND BLACK PEPPER

FOR THE SALMON TACOS:
1¼ LB WILD SALMON FILLET,
    ABOUT 1 INCH THICK
3 TBSP EXTRA-VIRGIN OLIVE OIL
2–3 TSP ANCHO, GUAJILLO, OR
    PASILLA OAXACA CHILI POWDER,
    ACCORDING TO PREFERENCE
¼ TSP KOSHER SALT
8 (6-INCH) CORN TORTILLAS,
    WARMED

Serves 4
Dairy-free
Gluten-free (if made with
100% corn tortillas)

Make the cabbage slaw:

1 In a medium bowl, toss together the cabbage and onion. Drizzle over the vinegar and oil, squeeze on the lime juice, and toss to blend. Sprinkle with salt and pepper to taste.

Make the salmon tacos:

2 Preheat a gas grill to 375°F. Slice the fillet into long strips about 2 inches wide.

3 In a medium bowl, combine the olive oil, chili powder, and salt. Add the salmon to the bowl and, using your fingers, rub the spice mixture thoroughly into the strips. Thread the strips onto metal skewers.

4 Set the salmon skewers on one side of the grill and cook for 4 minutes. Flip them over and grill another 3–4 minutes, until the salmon is just cooked through. After you flip the salmon, place the corn tortillas directly on the grates of the other side of the grill. Cook for about 1 minute per side—you want them still soft, but with a nice smoky grill flavor.

5 Let everyone build their own tacos using the slaw, the salmon, your favorite styles of salsa, wedges of lime, and any other taco garnishes you prefer.

AMY GRONDIN

Fishing Vessel DUNA

Amy Grondin means business. As a fisherman in both Washington and Alaska, she works incredibly hard during salmon season. Off-season, she works just as hard as a sustainable seafood consultant. The goals are fairly simple: have a financially successful season catching salmon the old-fashioned way, by hook and line, and follow that success with months of effective communication with chefs, seafood buyers, and fishermen about ways of protecting the ongoing health of the world's last wild salmon populations. The goals are simple, but achieving them is not.

Amy has been spending salmon season in Bristol Bay since 1993, when a whim led her to a seasonal job as a cook on a tender (a small boat that goes out to the fishing boats to purchase the day's catch). Some parts of the first year were tough, but as she learned to cope with seasickness, she got hooked. Imagine a pod of beluga whales bobbing in the waves like giant marshmallows, a crowd of bald eagles fighting over a school of fish, the daily cup of coffee at sunrise over the glowing Pacific—and these sights simply being part of your workday. After all these years, Amy still gets terribly seasick, but she loves being a fisherman.

Amy and her husband, Greg, bought their own boat for the 2011 season—*F/V Duna*, a sweet little craft with living quarters about the size of a throw pillow, and a powder blue John Deere engine. Their plan isn't that different from that of other fishing vessels in Puget Sound. They'll fish in local waters in May and, with luck and effort, they'll sell that catch and finance the fuel for the trip to Bristol Bay.

Before Amy ever set foot on a boat, she worked in restaurants, and she continued to work in restaurants during the off-season for a number of years. As a restaurant's resident fisherman, she naturally became the go-to staff person as fishery issues became more of a concern to both chefs and customers. She started paying more attention to sustainability, following the early progress of the Marine Stewardship Council and passing along information as the MSC began certifying sustainable fisheries. In the early years of these changes, fishermen were viewed as the enemy, an idea that's shifting as fishermen come to think of themselves as stewards of the oceans in much the same way that sustainable farmers think of themselves as land stewards.

That shift in perspective on the fishing vessels is partially due to Amy's work as a consultant for the Pacific Marine Conservation Council. She preaches a "3 H" approach: harvest, hatcheries, and habitat. Spawning streams—those local watershed projects all around Puget Sound—provide wild salmon with the right breeding environment. Hatchery programs boost overall population levels, as we grapple with the long-term effects of dams, pollution, and overfishing. Harvesting sets appropriate limits on the annual catch. Separately, none of these three points are effective; together, they might save our salmon. Rather than hopping onto a soapbox and proclaiming the evils of plastic bags, Amy smiles and feeds you coho she caught with her own capable hands. She describes the experience of fishing with gorgeous clarity and lets you directly experience the miracle of flavor that is wild salmon. It's easy to take these fish for granted—even if your household budget can afford only keta instead of the pricey chinook. If Amy has her way, there will never be a reason to buy farmed salmon. Instead, we'll be pitching in to restore salmon habitat, voting to maintain hatchery projects, and buying healthy salmon right off the boat.

SPRING SHELLFISH STEW WITH KALE AND PANCETTA

From Jess Thomson

This shellfish stew offers a nice bit of flexibility, depending on what's in season around town and what your fishmonger might have on special. If local mussels haven't come into season yet, double up the clams—or, just as easily, skip the clams and use all mussels. The shrimp are optional, and we urge you to include them only if you can find—and afford—wild-caught British Columbia or West Coast spot prawns, or U.S.-farmed freshwater prawns. Carefully sourcing your shellfish can be tedious, but it has critical importance. Our locally farmed clams and mussels are highly sustainable, but most farmed shrimp are raised in poor conditions that contribute to regional drought and the spread of disease to wild shrimp populations. Serve the stew with a simple green salad and good, crusty bread for mopping up the juices.

¼ LB PANCETTA, CUT INTO
   ¼-INCH CUBES
1 LARGE YELLOW ONION,
   HALVED AND THINLY SLICED
3 LARGE CLOVES GARLIC,
   FINELY CHOPPED
¼–½ TSP RED PEPPER FLAKES,
   TO TASTE
1 SMALL (ROUGHLY ½ LB) BUNCH
   KALE, STEMMED AND SLICED
   INTO ¼-INCH-THICK RIBBONS
SALT
FRESHLY GROUND BLACK PEPPER
2 CUPS DRY WHITE WINE
1 (28 OZ) CAN PEELED
   WHOLE TOMATOES
1 (8 OZ) BOTTLE CLAM JUICE

3 CUPS CHICKEN OR FISH STOCK
¾ LB MANILA CLAMS, SCRUBBED
   CLEAN
¾ LB MUSSELS, SCRUBBED CLEAN
   AND DEBEARDED IF NECESSARY
   (DISCARD ANY THAT ARE
   BROKEN OR WON'T CLOSE)
1 LB HALIBUT FILLET, CUT INTO
   1-INCH CUBES
¾ LB (ABOUT 12) EXTRA-LARGE
   SHRIMP, DEVEINED (OPTIONAL)
¼ CUP FINELY CHOPPED FRESH
   FLAT-LEAF PARSLEY

Serves 4
Dairy-free
Gluten-free

1 Heat a large, deep soup pot over medium heat. Add the pancetta, cover, and cook until browned, stirring frequently, about 10 minutes. Using a slotted spoon, transfer the pancetta to a paper towel–lined plate, leaving the fat in the pot.

2 Add the onion to the pot and cook until soft, about 10 minutes, stirring occasionally. Add the garlic, red pepper, and kale, season to taste with salt and pepper, and cook for another 10 minutes, stirring and turning as the kale on the bottom cooks down.

3 Increase the heat to high, add the wine, and simmer for 2 minutes.

4 Use your hands to break the tomatoes into small pieces and add them, along with their juices, and the clam juice, stock, and pancetta to the pot. Lower the heat to medium and simmer the stew, partially covered, until the kale is soft and the tomatoes begin to break down, about 30 minutes. (You can add a little water, if too much evaporates.) Season to taste with salt and pepper.

5 Add the clams and mussels to the pot and cook, tightly covered, for 5 minutes. Add the fish and shrimp, if using, stirring them into the broth, and simmer, covered, until the fish is cooked and all the shellfish have opened, another 5 minutes or so. Serve piping hot in bowls, sprinkled with the parsley. (Discard any clams or mussels that won't open.)

CHAPTER 4

SANDWICHES, SUPPERS, AND SNACKS

Maybe it's the influence of our nearby dairy farms, or maybe it's our love of all the new mobile food vendors around town, but we dearly love to graze. Quick one-pot meals, sandwiches loaded with local ingredients, sweet daytime tidbits like quick bread—each of these is so tasty it can make you forget the desire for more complicated dishes. These are recipes you'll use over and over again, tweaking them a bit to accommodate your home's flavor preferences or to more effectively use whatever your garden offers in abundance. In fact, we hope that you'll find inspiration here to whip up something that becomes uniquely your own. Be sure to pass your version around—that's how dishes become family classics.

DUNGENESS CRAB MELT

From Re:public Restaurant & Bar

There are two times each year when these sandwiches are entirely perfect. One is after a cold but successful day of crabbing somewhere on Puget Sound, and you're faced with the overwhelming thrill of a pile of clacking crustaceans. Break them down into picked-over meat and it's easily possible you'll want something cheesy and comforting for your supper. The second is whenever you spot a great deal on Dungeness around town—if you keep your eyes open, you'll find a few bargains every year. Sweet crab, sharp cheese, tangy sourdough, and just enough peppery kick to keep you awake—add a crunchy pickle and a cold lager and you, my friend, are dining like a king.

6 PIQUILLO PEPPERS
½ CUP MAYONNAISE
1 LB PICKED DUNGENESS CRAB
   MEAT
½ RED ONION, FINELY CHOPPED
2½ TBSP CHOPPED FRESH CILANTRO
½–1 TSP CHILI POWDER, TO TASTE
FRESH LEMON JUICE

SALT
FRESHLY GROUND BLACK PEPPER
8 SLICES SOURDOUGH BREAD
8 SLICES SHARP WHITE CHEDDAR
1 TBSP UNSALTED BUTTER

Makes 4 sandwiches

1 Preheat the oven to 400°F.

2 Puree the piquillo peppers in a food processor until smooth; then add the mayonnaise, and pulse until combined.

3 In a medium bowl, combine the crab, onion, and cilantro. Gently fold in the pepper mayonnaise until the crab is nicely coated. Add the chili powder and season to taste with lemon juice, salt, and black pepper.

4 Put a generous scoop of the crab salad on a slice of sourdough bread. Top with 2 slices of cheddar and another slice of sourdough.

5 Melt the butter in an ovenproof 12-inch sauté pan over medium-high heat. When the butter starts to foam, add the 4 sandwiches. Cook until the sandwiches are brown on their bottom sides. Flip each sandwich and remove the pan from the heat. Place the pan in the oven until the sandwiches are browned on their bottom sides and the cheese has melted.

BOAT STREET KITCHEN BACON SANDWICH

*From Susan Kaplan,
Boat Street Kitchen*

This is a simple sort of recipe that demands terrific ingredients. Happily, we live where it's easy to find great bread, great bacon, and great cheese. Boat Street Kitchen uses Columbia City Bakery mini baguettes, and they're an excellent choice. For cheese, try Beecher's Flagship or Appel Farms extra sharp—you want something with a touch of sourness to counteract the bacon. In regard to that bacon: the goal here is crisp, salty, smoky, heavily streaked, very American-style bacon. It's hard to go wrong with Sea Breeze Farm or Skagit River Ranch, or Hempler's thick-cut bacon, smoked in Ferndale.

The last crucial ingredient is the tomato. The richness of this sandwich necessitates a sharp, flavorful standout, which means this sandwich is at its best when homegrown tomatoes are available. If you don't have Roma, you can substitute another small, firm and meaty variety.

4 SLICES BACON
1 MINI BAGUETTE, OR ⅓ OF A
    FULL-SIZE BAGUETTE
1 TSP EXTRA-STRONG DIJON
    MUSTARD
¾ CUP GRATED EXTRA-SHARP
    CHEDDAR CHEESE

1–2 BEST-QUALITY ROMA TOMATOES
    YOU CAN FIND, SLICED
FRESHLY GROUND BLACK PEPPER

Makes 1 sandwich

1 Preheat the oven to 400°F. Fill a baking pan with water to the depth of 1 inch. Place wire baking racks over the water and set the slices of bacon on the rack so they don't overlap. Bake until the bacon is just a few moments short of ideal crispness, 14–18 minutes. This can be done several hours before you assemble the sandwich.

2 Preheat the oven to 375°F.

3 Cut the baguette in half lengthwise and spread both sides with a very thin layer of the mustard, making sure you cover the whole surface. Sprinkle half the cheese on each piece of bread, covering the mustard completely—a little might fall off, but try to mound it back on. Place the baguettes, topping side up, in a baking dish. Bake until bubbly and just starting to get golden around the outside edges, about 7 minutes. Once the cheese begins to melt, place the bacon in the oven on a heatproof dish to warm it, if necessary.

4 When the cheese is golden and crispy around the edges, remove the baguette halves from the oven and place tomato slices over each half so that they cover the surface but do not overlap. Season the tomatoes generously with pepper. Place 2 slices of bacon on each half, crisscrossing them. Serve open-faced, with a knife and fork for those who are fastidious.

Caution: This sandwich will be very hot. Let cool before serving to children, and warn adults.

DUCK EGG SANDWICH

*Adapted from David Krepky
by Becky Selengut*

This is as simple as a sandwich can be, and neither David nor Becky has any patience with people who want to fiddle with it. Don't be waylaid by hot sauce or tempted to add tomato slices: it's perfect as is. When Becky spent a couple of weeks with David and Cindy at Dog Mountain Farm, preparing for a duck-centric farm-to-table dinner, she ate this sandwich every single day. And with duck eggs becoming easier to find, it's possible that you might do the same.

Duck eggs have slightly more cholesterol in their yolks and slightly more albumen in their whites than chicken eggs have. So you'll find the yolk has a richer flavor and the white a firmer texture in comparison. Duck eggs are sold by Dog Mountain Farm and Sea Breeze Farm (look for them at farmers' markets) and Steibrs Farms as well (sold at PCC Natural Markets and Whole Foods).

Edible Tip

For this sandwich, we especially like to use a bread with a slight sweetness—either Columbia City Bakery's potato bread or Macrina's oatmeal buttermilk loaf.

2 TBSP UNSALTED BUTTER
1 DUCK EGG
2 SLICES OF YOUR FAVORITE BREAD
COPIOUS AMOUNTS OF
    MAYONNAISE, PREFERABLY
    BEST FOODS

SALT
FRESHLY GROUND BLACK PEPPER

Makes 1 sandwich

1 Heat a sauté pan over medium heat. Melt the butter, then crack the egg directly into the pan. Cover the pan.

2 While the egg cooks, cover each slice of bread with mayonnaise. Season one slice of bread with salt and pepper to taste.

3 Lift the lid on the pan, break the yolk (this will prevent some embarrassing orange goo stains later), cook for another 30 seconds, and place on your bread. Slap the two slices together to thoroughly smoosh the egg.

CRISPY CHILI SHRIMP SLIDERS

From Rachel Yang and Seif Chirchi, Joule

Rachel and Seif's food regularly sets the city to swooning with their swank-but-comfy Joule and the street-food palace Revel. This recipe came to us a few short weeks before the opening of Revel, and it's a glorious—and gloriously messy—treat where each bite hits you with a bit of heat, tanginess, and sweetness all in succession. A few of the ingredients provide a great excuse to wander around in the city's great Asian grocery stores: look for the steam buns and *gochujang* at Uwajimaya, H Mart, or Viet Wah. Accompany the sliders with some smoked pork belly from Rain Shadow Meats, seasonal pickles, and lime–condensed milk dip.

FOR THE SHRIMP:
¾ CUP ALL-PURPOSE FLOUR
¼ CUP RICE FLOUR
1 TBSP CORNSTARCH
SALT
FRESHLY GROUND BLACK PEPPER
RICE BRAN OIL FOR FRYING
8 HEAD-ON WILD-CAUGHT
  SPOT PRAWNS, SHELLED AND
  DEVEINED
2 TBSP GOCHUJANG (KOREAN CHILI
  PASTE)
1 TBSP MIRIN (RICE WINE)
1 TBSP RICE VINEGAR
1 TSP FISH SAUCE
1 TSP MINCED GARLIC
1 TSP PEELED AND MINCED FRESH
  GINGER

1 TSP SEEDED AND CHOPPED
  SERRANO CHILE
2 TSP MINCED SCALLION
¼ CUP CILANTRO LEAVES

FOR THE LIME–CONDENSED
MILK DIP:
½ CUP CONDENSED MILK
JUICE OF 1 LIME
1 TSP FRESHLY GROUND BLACK
  PEPPER
¼ TSP SALT
⅛ TSP CAYENNE PEPPER
4 STEAM BUNS

Serves 2

Prepare the shrimp:

1 In a broad, shallow bowl, combine the flours and cornstarch, and season with salt and pepper to taste.

2 Heat ¾ inch of rice bran oil in a large sauté pan to 375°F over medium-high heat. Dredge the prawns in the flour mixture and fry them in the hot oil until they are crispy, no more than a few minutes (depending on the size of the prawns). Place the cooked prawns on paper towels to drain.

3 In a medium bowl, mix the *gochujang*, mirin, rice vinegar, fish sauce, garlic, ginger, and serrano chile together. Add the fried prawns, scallion, and cilantro to the mixture and toss until well combined.

Make the lime–condensed milk dip:

4 In a small bowl, stir the condensed milk, lime juice, black pepper, salt, and cayenne together until well blended.

5 Serve the shrimp mixture with the steam buns and milk dip on the side as a condiment.

TARRAGON CHICKEN SALAD SANDWICHES

From Chef Buck, FareStart

Sometimes, good things come into our lives by sneaking in through the back door. The head chef at FareSart was visiting his parents in Toronto several years ago, and sous chef (and former FareStart student) Buck slipped this chicken salad sandwich on the menu. It was an instant hit, and Lieu was smart enough to keep it around, even though he has a strong resistance to the idea of "salad sandwiches." We tend to mix up a batch when we've got leftover fried or roast chicken—or, during the holidays, scraps of roast turkey. The basic flavors are straightforward, and the addition of apples and the Brie-style Cirrus cheese from Mt. Townsend Creamery lifts the sandwich into the realm of remarkable. FareStart uses potato or sourdough bread—and while that's delicious, it's just as great on whatever sort of sandwich bread is your favorite.

1 LB CHOPPED COOKED CHICKEN
   THIGH OR BREAST MEAT
2 CELERY STALKS, FINELY DICED
½ SMALL RED ONION, FINELY DICED
2 TBSP MINCED FRESH TARRAGON
JUICE AND GRATED ZEST OF
   ½ LEMON
2 TBSP DIJON MUSTARD
SALT
FRESHLY GROUND BLACK PEPPER
⅔–1 CUP MAYONNAISE, TO TASTE
8 SLICES GOOD BREAD
12 THIN SLICES TART APPLE,
   PLUS MORE FOR SERVING
8 THIN SLICES MT. TOWNSEND
   CIRRUS CHEESE

Makes 4 sandwiches

1 In a medium bowl, combine the chicken, celery, onion, and tarragon. Toss in the lemon juice and zest and stir in the mustard. Season with salt and pepper to taste. Stir in the mayonnaise a small amount at a time, until the salad is bound together to your liking. Taste and adjust the seasonings again as necessary.

2 Place a scoop of chicken salad on a slice of your favorite sandwich bread. Top with 3 slices of apple, 2 slices of Cirrus cheese, and the second slice of bread. Serve with additional apple slices.

RENÉ FEATHERSTONE AND LENA LENTZ HARDT

Lentz Spelt Farm

Recent generations of Americans are used to thinking of wheat as a faceless commodity—we might sing about amber waves of grain, but few of us have actually seen a wheat field. René Featherstone likes to point out that our massive agricultural commodity system works both ways: few wheat farmers have any direct connection to their customers. René and Lena Lentz Hardt work a little differently.

René and Lena are partners in Lentz Spelt Farms, but they don't call themselves farmers, and they don't suggest alternative job titles. Lena spends her days dealing with the paperwork pertaining to both accounting and organic certification, and makes all the decisions concerning the farm's agricultural programs. René divides his time between sales and field consulting, which can involve anything from estimating crop yields to protein analysis. Like all small producers, they both spend a lot of time on the phone, but the actual guy driving the tractor on the field is a young neighbor. He's the farmer. René and Lena are something else.

Lena's family has owned the land in Marlin since Teddy Roosevelt signed the Homestead Act Certificate back in 1906, a certificate that still hangs in Lena's farmhouse. These 880 acres on the Columbia Plateau are arid, getting fewer than 8 inches of rain in a year. The plateau's dry summer heat and alkaline soil make it a world-class wheat-growing region—one that isn't that different from the Fertile Crescent, where agriculture first came into being thousands of years ago. Perhaps it's not surprising that when Lena and René wanted to shift away from the commodity system, they looked to ancient grains to supply the answer.

Their first crop was spelt, an ancestor of modern wheat. They purchased two kinds from an Ohio seed company and, in 2000, they signed a contract with a small Oregon flour mill. The volume of the contract was larger than they could grow on their 240 arable acres, so they in turn contracted out a portion to another farm. The volume has grown since then, but the model is the same. They now work with six farms to fulfill the spelt needs of the Oregon mill, and every year before harvest, Rene and Lena meet with the growers to develop a bushel price.

After the first year's success with spelt, they bought emmer seed of the same genetically pure quality as their spelt. Lena's field in Marlin was Washington's first emmer crop, and the following year they contracted with two more farms to grow it. Emmer has since become a common sight on restaurant menus, served as a whole grain that's been cooked slowly in broth.

As the market for spelt and emmer continued to grow, Lena and Rene took on a fascinating, slow-developing project that reached production only in 2010. Their einkorn field began as only a few grams of seed. Over 6 years, they cosseted these grains along, even placing protection sleeves on some of the grain heads, until they had enough to plant a production field in 2009. In the winter of 2010–2011, einkorn became available on a very limited basis. It has a fine, nutty flavor that's similar to that of emmer, but it's a softer grain and cooks much more quickly.

Okay, so they insist they're not technically farmers. Whatever they are, we can only hope that they'll convince more commodity producers to join them in their suspiciously farmer-like agricultural research and their direct-sales business model, so we can reap the delicious whole-grain benefit.

FIELD ROAST REUBEN

From FareStart

This tasty sandwich has been on the FareStart menu for years, and it quietly points to a relationship that dates back to the beginnings of both the grain meat company and the nonprofit education program. In 1992, Chef David Lee converted his Common Meals company to a nonprofit organization that provided culinary job training to Seattle's homeless. Five years later, he created Field Roast, still based in the International District. Common Meals is now FareStart, a gorgeous downtown lunch spot that offers an incredible array of education and services to homeless and disadvantaged citizens. Meanwhile, Field Roast has gone from a few simple grain meat loaves to a product line that includes sausages, holiday roasts, pâtés, and deli slices. It tastes nothing like pastrami—but that doesn't mean it's not tasty.

Edible Tip

FareStart's Guest Chef Nights are not just a good deal—they're your weekly chance to dine out for a great cause. One of greater Seattle's best chefs comes through this kitchen every Thursday night, serving up a 3-course meal for about $20. While you're enjoying dinner, students are getting the chance to work with talented leaders and make connections that can lead to great jobs down the line. See FareStart.org for more details.

2 SLICES MARBLE, LIGHT, OR DARK
    RYE BREAD
UNSALTED BUTTER
2 TBSP THOUSAND ISLAND
    DRESSING
2 OZ SAUERKRAUT

2 SLICES GRUYÈRE CHEESE
4 OZ SMOKED TOMATO DELI-SLICED
    FIELD ROAST

Makes 1 sandwich
Vegetarian

1 Coat one side of each slice of rye evenly—but not too thickly—with butter. Place one slice of bread butter side down in a cast-iron or nonstick skillet, and place the skillet over low heat. Coat the bread with the Thousand Island dressing and top with the sauerkraut, Gruyère, and Field Roast slices. Cover with the remaining slice of buttered rye, so the buttered side faces up.

2 Slowly brown each side of the sandwich, carefully flipping it over from time to time. Serve when the cheese is melted and the bread is grilled to your liking.

PORK BANH MI

Montreal has smoked meat. Philadelphia has its cheesesteak. New York owns the hot pastrami on rye. New Orleans gets two: the po' boy and the muffaletta. We think Seattle needs a definitive sandwich, and we think it should be the banh mi. We issue halfhearted apologies if you feel like Saigon should retain sandwich rights. New York didn't invent pastrami on rye, either. A great banh mi starts with the right kind of bread. Lots of artisan bakeries around town make excellent baguettes, but for this you need Vietnamese sandwich-sized baguettes from a Vietnamese bakery. They are legion across South Seattle: all along Martin Luther King Jr. Way (Q Bakery at Graham Street is a favorite), on Sixteenth Avenue in White Center, or in Little Saigon, centered on Twelfth and Jackson. Pick up the daikon and condiments at Viet Wah, and everything else can be found all summer long at your farmers' market.

Edible Tips

If you're using pork from other ranchers, look for a lean cut that is boneless and thinly sliced, or buy thin boneless chops and trim the fat yourself.

If you rely on your closest grocery store to supply you with the right bread, the best approximation will be the skinniest store-brand baguette you can find in the bakery department. The thin, shattering crust is key, as is the contrast with a fluffy interior.

FOR THE PICKLED VEGETABLES:
½ CUP SHREDDED OR JULIENNED CARROTS
½ CUP SHREDDED DAIKON RADISH
1 TBSP MIRIN
1 TBSP RICE VINEGAR
PINCH OF KOSHER SALT

FOR THE SANDWICHES:
1 TBSP FISH SAUCE
1 TBSP SOY SAUCE
½ TSP SRIRACHA HOT SAUCE
½ TSP SUGAR

KOSHER SALT
FRESHLY GROUND BLACK PEPPER
1 LB SKAGIT RIVER RANCH STIR-FRY PORK
4 VIETNAMESE SANDWICH BAGUETTES
SOY MAYONNAISE
1 SMALL CUCUMBER, JULIENNED
1 JALAPEÑO PEPPER, THINLY SLICED ON THE BIAS (OPTIONAL)
16 SPRIGS FRESH CILANTRO

Makes 4 sandwiches

Make the pickled vegetables:

1 In a small bowl, combine the carrots and daikon. Gently stir in the mirin, vinegar, and salt. Cover and let marinate at room temperature for 30 minutes.

Make the sandwiches:

2 Preheat a gas grill to 400°F.

3 Combine the fish sauce, soy sauce, hot sauce, sugar, salt, and pepper in a small bowl. Lay the thin slices of pork on a baking sheet and brush both sides with the marinade. Thread the pieces of pork loosely onto metal skewers, so the meat gets gentle pleats in each piece. Grill until the pork is nicely crisp along the thinner edges, about 4 minutes per side.

4 Using an oven mitt to protect your hand from the hot skewer, pull the pork off onto a cutting board. Chop the pork into roughly bite-size pieces. Let the pork cool slightly while you finish prepping.

5 Slice the baguettes lengthwise, leaving one long end uncut. Spread both sides of the bread lightly with mayonnaise. Fill each roll with one-quarter of the chopped pork and top with one-quarter of the pickled vegetables. Add several pieces of cucumber to each sandwich and, if desired, a few jalapeño slices. Finish each sandwich with 4 sprigs of cilantro and a few grinds of fresh black pepper.

BROWN SUGAR–RHUBARB BREAD

*Adapted from a recipe
by Lanne Stauffer*

Seattle is just up the road from Sumner, the self-proclaimed Rhubarb Pie Capital of the world, and while we may not have the colorful commercial rhubarb fields of our South Sound neighbor, it does seem like most of our backyards contain a rhubarb plant. When rhubarb is fresh, pie is a splendid use for it, but we wanted to find better uses for "pie plant" once it's been sliced and frozen. A dear friend and excellent baker from Ballard (she's better known as an owner of Market Street Shoes) happens to make the world's greatest banana bread, made from bananas straight out of the freezer. She was kind enough to fork over her recipe, and we proceeded to tinker around with the method and ingredients adjusted for frozen rhubarb. The result is a cake-like bread where the tart rhubarb and sweet brown sugar play off each other perfectly.

1 STICK (8 TBSP) UNSALTED BUTTER

2 CUPS SLICED FROZEN RHUBARB, PLUS ½ CUP FINELY DICED FROZEN RHUBARB

1¼ CUPS FIRMLY PACKED DARK BROWN SUGAR

2 LARGE EGGS

½ CUP MILK

½ TSP VANILLA EXTRACT

2½ CUPS ALL-PURPOSE FLOUR

1 TSP BAKING SODA

1 TSP SALT

Makes 2 loaves

1 Preheat the oven to 350°F. Butter either an 8 x 4-inch loaf pan or a 9 x 5-inch loaf pan.

2 In a microwave-safe medium bowl, combine the butter and the 2 cups frozen rhubarb slices. Cook in the microwave on high until the butter is very soft and nearly melted, anywhere from 45 seconds to 2 minutes. Use a wooden spoon to blend slightly. (The butter won't combine very much with the water from the rhubarb.) Add the brown sugar and stir until well mixed. Beat in the eggs one at a time; then stir in milk and vanilla until well incorporated. Sprinkle the flour, baking soda, and salt on top of the wet ingredients and blend until the batter becomes smooth, with a few air holes. Gently fold in the finely diced rhubarb. Divide the batter evenly between the two prepared loaf pans.

3 Bake until the tops of the loaves are a deep brown and a tester inserted into the center of each comes out clean, 60–70 minutes. Set on a wire rack and cool in the pans for 30 minutes. Run a thin metal spatula or knife around the outside to release the loaves from their pans. The bread can be eaten while still warm, or left to cool before slicing.

Edible Tip

The easiest way to freeze rhubarb when it's in season is to simply slice the stalks into 1-inch-thick pieces. You can either lay them on a baking sheet and pour the frozen pieces into a storage bag once they're frozen, or simply pour the raw chunks directly into the freezer bag, where a few might stick together as they freeze. To convert the ½ cup into finely diced pieces, just use a heavy chef's knife to slice each frozen piece into four or five smaller pieces—the general small size is important, rather than a precisely square dice.

SANDWICHES, SUPPERS, AND SNACKS

CHERRY AND ROSEMARY FOCACCIA

From Lara Ferroni

This is a treat when it's cherry season. Cherries are an important crop for Washington, and during June and July you can expect that even grocery store cherries are grown nearby. The problem is that different varieties are packed in the same bag all season, so "sweet red cherries" can vary greatly from week to week when you buy them in the supermarket.

To try out specific types, head to the farmers' markets to find Chelan, Bing, Van, Lambert, Skeena, Sweetheart, and Lapin varieties, each with a slightly different sweetness and flavor. The supersized Tieton is the only sweet cherry that doesn't work well in this recipe—they're so big that they can actually interfere with how the bread bakes.

This is a particularly handy recipe if you're lucky enough to have a backyard tree. Since you need just two cups of cherries, it's quick work to gather them before the birds move in.

FOR THE DOUGH:
1½ TSP ACTIVE DRY YEAST
1 TBSP SUGAR
¼ CUP OLIVE OIL, PLUS MORE
   FOR OILING THE BOWL
1 TSP SALT
4 CUPS ALL-PURPOSE FLOUR

FOR THE TOPPING:
1 TSP OLIVE OIL
2 CUPS PITTED FRESH SWEET
   CHERRIES, HALVED

FLAKE OR COARSE SEA SALT
FINELY GRATED ZEST FROM
   1 LEMON
LEAVES FROM SEVERAL SPRIGS
   FRESH ROSEMARY
HONEY FOR BRUSHING

Makes 4 (5-inch) rounds
Vegetarian
Dairy-free

1 Mix the yeast, sugar, and 1¼ cups warm water in the bowl of a stand mixer fitted with the whisk attachment. Give a quick stir and set aside for about 5 minutes to proof.

2 Stir in the olive oil and salt. Mix in the flour 1 cup at a time. When all the flour has been mixed in, switch to the dough hook if you have one or transfer the dough from the mixer bowl to a floured work surface and start kneading by hand. Mix or knead until the dough is shiny and firm (about 3 minutes in the mixer and 12 minutes by hand). Then knead by hand, adding more flour if the dough is sticky, for another 5 minutes.

3 Lightly oil a large bowl and place the dough in the bowl, turning once to coat with the oil. Cover the bowl with plastic wrap or a damp towel, and set in a warm place to rise for at least 1 hour. The dough should approximately double in size.

4 Punch down the dough and divide into 4 pieces. On a floured work surface, flatten each piece and roll out to about a 4-inch round. Flip the dough over and press it lightly all over with your fingertips to make little dimples in it. Flip the dough and repeat. Do this 2 or 3 more times. Then place it on a baking sheet.

5 Lightly brush each round of dough with the olive oil; then cover them with the cherries, skin side up, gently pushing each cherry half into the dough a touch, being careful not to crush it. Sprinkle the dough with the sea salt, lemon zest, and rosemary. Cover with plastic again and let sit in a warm place for 20–30 minutes.

6 While the breads are having their final rise, preheat the oven to 400°F. Remove the plastic and bake on the center rack for 15 minutes. Remove from the oven, drizzle well with honey, and use a pastry brush to coat the crust edges. Return to the oven and bake until the crust is a light golden brown, about another 5 minutes.

7 Remove from the oven, drizzle with a bit more honey, and sprinkle on a little more salt. Let cool for about 10 minutes before slicing into wedges or strips.

SUGAR HUBBARD SPICE LOAF

The Sugar Hubbard grown by Sherman's Pioneer Farm Produce on Whidbey Island is a unique heritage squash (it was added to the Slow Food Ark of Taste in 2011) we love to celebrate. Nearly big enough to serve as Cinderella's coach, the Sugar Hubbard has a lumpy, blue-gray outside, but its sweet, meaty interior puts the popular Sugar Pie pumpkin to shame. You might be skeptical that a squash merits this praise; heck, we were skeptical ourselves. Then we roasted some, had a taste, and lost our minds. This squash really is something special.

The Shermans grow the only commercial crop of Sugar Hubbard in existence, which means it's not as easy to find as we'd like—and once it's gone for the year, it's gone. The best way of solving the supply problem, aside from growing it yourself (you can order seeds from the Territorial Seed Catalog), is to roast a mountain of it in the fall and freeze small tubs of the puree until you're in the mood to bake.

We will grudgingly admit that this recipe does fine if you substitute either canned pumpkin or roasted Sugar Pie pumpkin.

2 CUPS ALL-PURPOSE FLOUR
1 TSP GROUND CINNAMON
¼ TSP GROUND ALLSPICE
¼ TSP GROUND CARDAMOM
⅛ TSP GROUND CLOVES
1 TSP BAKING SODA
½ TSP SALT
1½ CUPS PUREED ROASTED SUGAR
     HUBBARD SQUASH
½ CUP GRANULATED SUGAR

½ CUP FIRMLY PACKED
     BROWN SUGAR
1 STICK (8 TBSP) UNSALTED
     BUTTER, MELTED AND COOLED
½ TSP VANILLA EXTRACT
2 LARGE EGGS

Makes 1 loaf
Vegetarian

1 Preheat the oven to 350°F. Grease an 8 by 4-inch loaf pan or a 9 x 5-inch loaf pan and set aside.

2 In a small mixing bowl, blend together the flour, cinnamon, allspice, cardamom, cloves, baking soda, and salt. In a large bowl, stir together the squash puree, both sugars, melted butter, vanilla, and eggs. Add the dry ingredients all at once, stir until mixed thoroughly, and pour into the prepared loaf pan.

3 Bake until a toothpick inserted into the middle comes out clean, about 1 hour. Cool for 30 minutes; then gently loosen the sides from the pan and place on a cooling rack for another hour before slicing.

EINKORN AND BEAN MINESTRONE

From Eliza Ward, ChefShop.com

Although we think of minestrone as a chunky vegetable soup with pasta, in Italy they often add whole emmer (farro) as the starch, instead of pasta. This version tweaks that tradition slightly, using a delicious grain called einkorn. Einkorn is one of the earliest domesticated types of wheat—evidence shows it was grown in the Fertile Crescent about 11,000 years ago, and it was found in the pockets of the famous Ötzi the Iceman in the Italian Alps. The Lentz Spelt Farm in Marlin harvested Washington's first commercial einkorn crop in 2010. It has a nutty flavor that's similar to emmer, but it has much smaller, softer grains, so it cooks more quickly. *Note:* the beans must be soaked overnight in advance.

Edible Tip

The Lentz einkorn crop is the first commercial einkorn crop grown in the United States, and it's still in limited supply. You can get 50-pound bags direct from the farm or buy 1-pound bags from ChefShop (see Resources, page 162).

2 TBSP EXTRA-VIRGIN OLIVE OIL, PLUS MORE FOR SERVING
1 MEDIUM ONION, CHOPPED
3 CARROTS, CHOPPED
2 STALKS CELERY, CHOPPED
3 CLOVES GARLIC, MINCED
¼ CUP SAUVIGNON BLANC OR AGRODOLCE WINE VINEGAR
2 FRESH TOMATOES, PEELED AND CHOPPED, OR ONE 14 OZ CAN SAN MARZANO TOMATOES, DRAINED
3 FRESH SAGE LEAVES
2 SPRIGS FRESH MARJORAM
½ LB DRIED WHITE BEANS, SOAKED IN COLD WATER TO COVER OVERNIGHT AND DRAINED
4 CUPS VEGETABLE STOCK
SEA SALT
FRESHLY GROUND BLACK PEPPER
1½ CUPS EINKORN
GRATED PARMIGIANO-REGGIANO, FOR SERVING

Serves 4
Vegetarian

1 In a stockpot over medium-low heat, warm the olive oil; then add the onion, carrots, celery, and garlic and cook, stirring a few times, for 5 minutes. Sprinkle the mixture with the vinegar and cook until it has been absorbed, another 5–10 minutes. Add the tomatoes, sage, and marjoram and simmer, stirring occasionally, for 15 minutes.

2 Add the drained beans and stock. Raise the heat to medium-high and bring to a boil; then reduce the heat and simmer for 50–60 minutes.

3 Season the mixture generously with salt and pepper, add the einkorn, and simmer until the einkorn is al dente and the beans are cooked through, another 30–40 minutes.

4 To serve, drizzle with olive oil and sprinkle with a little Parmigiano-Reggiano cheese.

GRAND MARNIER PRAWNS

From Bobby Moore, Barking Frog

With a citrusy-sweet mayonnaise that can be made well ahead of time, these fried prawns are a finger-licking midwinter supper. Wild-caught spot prawns are available from October to January (prices are usually best in fall). Be careful not to overcook them—it can happen in a flash. If you like to experiment with citrus, try hunting down a fresh yuzu. It's the only citrus that can grow this far north, and Wade Bennett at Rockridge Orchards sells the hazardously thorny plants for home gardens (he suggests that when planted under bedroom windows, they make an excellent deterrent to teens who might be tempted to sneak out). Add a few ounces of yuzu juice to the orange juice at the end of its reduction time, and the orange syrup will have an extra kick of light acidity. Uwajimaya occasionally has imported yuzu, but it's pricey enough to reserve for yuzu lemonade, where its flavor shines.

FOR THE GRAND MARNIER MAYONNAISE:
1 CUP GRAND MARNIER
4 CUPS ORANGE JUICE
3 TBSP DRIED ORANGE ZEST GROUND TO FINE DUST IN A COFFEE GRINDER
2 CUPS MAYONNAISE

FOR THE PRAWNS:
1 QT CANOLA OIL FOR DEEP FRYING
20 (ABOUT 2 LB) WILD-CAUGHT SPOT PRAWNS
1½ CUPS CORNSTARCH

Serves 4

1 Heat a small saucepan over medium heat and add the Grand Marnier to burn off some of the alcohol. Don't reduce the liquid further. Once the alcohol fumes burn off, remove the pan from the heat immediately.

2 In a separate pan over medium-low heat, reduce the orange juice to a syrup until about ½ cup is left. Cool; then combine with the Grand Marnier and orange zest powder. Chill until completely cold; then combine with the mayonnaise. Keep refrigerated until serving.

3 Heat the canola oil to 350°F in a Dutch oven over medium-high heat. Dredge the prawns in the cornstarch, shaking off any excess. Fry the prawns in small batches until crispy, about 2 minutes, and drain on paper towels.

4 In a large bowl, toss the hot prawns in the Grand Marnier mayonnaise to coat. Serve immediately.

OYSTER STEW

From Joe Michael

The most common, most inexpensive oyster around here is the Pacific, and it's pretty plain as oysters go. Oyster lovers won't turn their noses up at it, but rarely is it anyone's favorite. This recipe is an old-fashioned stew that takes the simple fact of inexpensive oysters for granted. The man behind it has raised his own oysters for a decade on Bainbridge Island. As it turns out, it's not hard work. "You come down, plant your oysters, and drink a beer. Three months later you come down, flip the bag, and drink another beer," says Joe. If this sounds appealing and you're lucky enough to have a spot of waterfront property, the joys of homegrown oysters can be yours, too. If you live on Bainbridge, check the Puget Sound Restoration Fund; elsewhere, you can buy seed oysters and supplies from Taylor Shellfish (see Resources, page 162).

4 CUPS HALF-AND-HALF
1 PT SHUCKED OYSTERS
   AND THEIR LIQUOR
1 TBSP UNSALTED BUTTER
½ CUP DICED CELERY
½ CUP DICED ONION
1 TSP CELERY SEEDS
1 TBSP FRESH LEMON JUICE

2 TBSP CHOPPED FRESH PARSLEY,
   CHERVIL, OR CHIVES, OR
   A MIXTURE OF ALL 3
SALT
FRESHLY GROUND BLACK PEPPER

Serves 4
Gluten-free

1 In a heavy 2-quart saucepan over medium heat, bring the half-and-half and oyster liquor to a simmer, reserving the oysters in a separate dish. Remove from the heat.

2 Meanwhile, in a large sauté pan over medium heat, melt the butter. Add the celery and cook, stirring, for 3–4 minutes. Add the onion and continue to cook, stirring, until translucent, 4–5 minutes. Add the celery seeds and oysters and cook until the edges of the oysters start to curl, 1–2 minutes.

3 Carefully transfer the oysters to a blender and add enough of the heated cream mixture just to cover. Puree the mixture until smooth. Pour the puree back into the saucepan and return the saucepan to medium heat until just heated through.

4 Just before serving, stir in the lemon juice and chopped herbs, and season with salt and pepper to taste.

Edible Tips

Pacific oysters can grow to substantial sizes—like that of an average adult foot. If you stumble across some of these monsters (or find a good deal), the easiest way to cook them properly is to give them a rough chop to about the size of a "two-bite" oyster. Make sure to reserve all the liquor for the stew.

If you're wondering what to drink alongside your stew and want something a little fancier than a cold beer, check out the results from the annual oyster wine competition (OysterWine.com), sponsored by Taylor Shellfish. Geared toward great wines to pair with raw oysters, they'll also work nicely with this stew.

CAVA AND CHORIZO STEAMED MUSSELS

From Mike Easton, Lecosho

Seattle is lucky to have two mussel options from our local shellfish farms: the well-adapted Mediterranean mussel and our native Penn Cove variety, which are acclaimed for their sweet, firm meat. Mussels take just a few minutes to cook, and considering that they're at their finest during the summer months (after spawning season), it's a terrific choice for a midsummer supper. A big part of mussel enjoyment comes from the sauce that typically accompanies them. This one has a lovely balance of spice and lightness, and you'll want to have plenty of warm, crusty baguette slices on hand to mop up every drop.

¼ CUP OLIVE OIL

2 TBSP CHOPPED GARLIC

3 OZ DRY-CURED CHORIZO, THINLY SLICED ON A SLANT

1 LB MUSSELS, SCRUBBED AND DEBEARDED IF NECESSARY

2 TBSP CHOPPED FENNEL FRONDS

¾ CUP CAVA OR OTHER DRY SPARKLING WINE

5 TBSP UNSALTED BUTTER

SEA SALT

Serves 2

Gluten-free (if served with gluten-free bread)

1 In a large saucepan, combine the olive oil, garlic, and chorizo. Place the pan over medium heat and lightly sauté the mixture for 2–3 minutes. Do not let the garlic brown.

2 Add the mussels to the pan and raise the heat slightly. Stir often. As the mussels start to open, add the chopped fennel and Cava. Raise the temperature to high for 1 minute, being sure the Cava comes to a simmer. Add the butter and stir until completely incorporated. Season with salt to taste.

3 Ladle into shallow bowls and serve immediately with plenty of good bread.

Edible Tip

Finding dry-cured chorizo isn't always easy in a town where the standard chorizo is the fresh seasoned Mexican product. Pike Place Market is a good bet, with DeLaurenti and Spanish Table both frequently offering multiple options.

CREAMY POLENTA
WITH ROASTED FOREST MUSHROOMS

From Lisa K. Nakamura,
Allium Restaurant

Our farmers' market season kicks off around Easter and extends until Thanksgiving, but the earliest and latest markets of the year can be a little unsatisfying if you're looking for a huge range of produce. Thankfully, chickens and ducks produce at least some eggs year-round, and spring and fall are great times for wild mushrooms. The typical weather that accompanies these times of year coincides beautifully with the right weather for this dish. It starts with creamy herbed polenta, which can be made several days in advance. When it's time for brunch or a cozy supper, reheat the polenta with more cream and top it with roasted mushrooms, gooey cheese, and an oozy sunny-side-up egg. You'll likely want a crisp green salad or some fresh seasonal fruit on the side to lighten things up, and a mimosa is the perfect liquid accompaniment.

Edible Tip

Lisa uses a mix of wild mushrooms to make this dish at Allium—and happily it's delicious with almost any kind of mushroom, either domesticated or wild. Use chopped portobello or crimini from the grocery store or splurge with morels or chanterelles when they're in season. To find wild mushrooms, see Resources, page 162.

3–4 CUPS WHOLE MILK (YOU CAN USE LOW-FAT MILK OR SOY MILK IF YOU LIKE)
1 TSP CRUSHED DRIED SAGE LEAVES OR 2 TSP CHOPPED FRESH SAGE
1 CLOVE GARLIC, FINELY MINCED
SALT
FRESHLY GROUND BLACK PEPPER
1 CUP FINE POLENTA
1 CUP HEAVY CREAM
3 TBSP UNSALTED BUTTER

1 LB MUSHROOMS, CHOPPED INTO BITE-SIZE PIECES
1 SPRIG FRESH THYME
4 LARGE EGGS (DUCK OR CHICKEN)
1 (5½ OZ) WHEEL MT. TOWNSEND CREAMERY CIRRUS OR OTHER CAMEMBERT
CHOPPED FRESH CHIVES FOR GARNISH (OPTIONAL)

Serves 4

1 In a large pot, bring the milk to a boil. Add the sage and garlic, season with some salt and pepper, then pour in the polenta. You should season the polenta while it is cooking, so try to estimate how much salt the finished dish will need. If you are not sure, be conservative with your guess. Stir the polenta constantly. When it has thickened, remove it from the heat. (You can make the polenta up to 3 days ahead; let cool and then store, covered, in the refrigerator.)

2 Preheat the oven to 350°F. In an oven-safe casserole, combine the cooked polenta, cream, and 1 cup water. Let the polenta heat up in the oven, stirring it every 5 minutes or so. (Don't worry if it gets brown and crispy; that just makes the polenta taste better.) Taste for seasoning, and add more salt and pepper as needed. Let it cook in the oven for 15–20 minutes.

3 While the polenta is in the oven, melt 1 tablespoon of the butter in an oven-safe sauté pan over medium-high heat; then add the mushrooms and cook, stirring, for several minutes. Season to taste with salt and pepper. Add the sprig of thyme, remove from the heat, and place the pan in the oven with the polenta.

4 Melt the remaining 2 tablespoons butter in a large sauté pan over medium heat. Gently crack the eggs into the melted butter, being careful not to break the yolks. Cook slowly until the whites are set and the yolk is firm but still soft, about 90 seconds. Remove the pan from the heat immediately.

5 To serve, divide the polenta among 4 shallow bowls. Add some of the roasted mushrooms and a slice of the Cirrus cheese. Top with one egg sunny-side up and sprinkle with chives.

SANDWICHES, SUPPERS, AND SNACKS

SHAKSHOUKA

Tomatoes are something of a gateway drug for farmers' market shoppers. Before diving into the unfamiliar world of romanesco or breakfast radishes, market newbies make a beeline for Billy's Tomatoes ("grown in sunny Okanogan") and pick up a few pounds of their heirloom varieties. But sooner or later, the week comes when it's pouring down rain in Seattle, while the sun still shines in Okanogan. We want something warm for dinner, something a little cozier than another plate of tomatoes drizzled with olive oil. Shakshouka is the answer. The dish comes to Seattle by way of Tunisia and parts of the Fertile Crescent—the regions that inspire Maria Hines's Golden Beetle restaurant and serve as the native cuisine for many South Seattle residents. The name means "all mixed up," and that's exactly what it is: ingredients from the New World and the Old, diced up and stewed, and topped with whatever sounds tasty.

Edible Tip

Many kinds of fresh heirloom tomatoes have thick skins that, when cooked, turn into stiff little quills that wreck the texture of the sauce. Unless you're sure that your favorite fresh tomato doesn't do this, we urge you to either take the time to blanch and peel your tomatoes or simply use canned ones.

¼ CUP EXTRA-VIRGIN OLIVE OIL
1 LARGE WHITE ONION, DICED
3 CLOVES GARLIC, MINCED
2 RED BELL PEPPERS, SEEDED AND DICED
1 JALAPEÑO PEPPER (OPTIONAL), SEEDED AND MINCED
1 TBSP PAPRIKA
1 TSP TURMERIC
3 CUPS PEELED AND DICED FRESH TOMATOES, OR 36 OZ CANNED DICED TOMATOES, WITH THEIR JUICE
1½ CUPS CHICKEN OR VEGETABLE BROTH
SALT
FRESHLY GROUND BLACK PEPPER
WARM PITA BREAD FOR SERVING

Serves 4
Vegan (if made with vegetable broth)
Gluten-free (if served on its own)

1 In a large saucepan over medium-high heat, warm the olive oil. Add the onion and cook, stirring, for several minutes until translucent and pale gold. Lower the temperature to medium-low, add the garlic, and cook for several more minutes, being careful not to brown the garlic.

2 Stir in the red peppers, jalapeño, paprika, and turmeric, blending well to make sure the spices don't clump. Cook for 5 minutes, stirring occasionally. Add the tomatoes (with their liquid, if using canned) and broth and stir to blend. Simmer, uncovered, until the liquids have reduced to a thick sauce, about 30 minutes. Taste and season with salt and black pepper as desired.

3 Serve hot with warm pita if desired. The basic sauce is delicious on its own, or you can top it with feta cheese, extra *za'atar*, poached eggs, sardines, crumbled sausage, or any combination that sounds appealing.

SAUSAGE ROLLS

From Amy Broomhall

Ever since Grand Central Bakery came out with their own frozen puff pastry, we've been playing around with these buttery, flaky, preposterously fattening sheets and have proven conclusively that everything but an old shoe tastes good if it's been wrapped in puff pastry. These tangy, meaty Australian sausage rolls are a Christmas tradition at Amy's house, although she usually uses ground turkey. Since it's currently impossible to find farmers' market ground turkey—and hey, we're already using puff pastry, so why worry about fat?—we stick with Aussie-style tradition and use ground pork, beef, or a mixture of the two. Pork's our favorite, but these rolls are great under all circumstances. They're a great snack to have on hand when kids are around (yes, sausage rolls go great with ketchup) or you're throwing a casual open house party—they're simple, filling, and tasty either hot or at room temperature.

Edible Tip

For unseasoned ground pork, look for Skagit River Ranch, Samish Bay, Olsen Farms, or Wooly Pigs at the farmers' markets. The first three ranches also sell ground beef.

2 FULL SHEETS FROZEN OR
  HOMEMADE PUFF PASTRY
2 SLICES STALE (OR VERY CRUSTY)
  BREAD
¼ CUP MILK
1 SMALL ONION, QUARTERED
4 CLOVES GARLIC, PEELED
1 TBSP WORCESTERSHIRE SAUCE
2 TBSP DIJON MUSTARD
3 TBSP TOMATO PASTE

1 TSP SALT
½ TSP FRESHLY GROUND
  BLACK PEPPER
½ TSP CURRY POWDER
½ TSP CELERY SEEDS
1½ LB GROUND PORK OR
  A MIX OF BEEF AND PORK

Makes 54 small rolls

1 Preheat the oven to 400°F. Line 2 baking sheets with parchment paper. While the oven is heating and you make the filling, defrost the puff pastry according to the directions.

2 In a food processor, pulse the bread into fine crumbs. In a large bowl, combine the crumbs with the milk to form a panada. Combine the onion and garlic in the food processor and pulse until the mixture is very smooth. Stir this into the bread panada until well mixed. Stir in the Worcestershire, mustard, tomato paste, salt, pepper, curry powder, and celery seeds. Finally, crumble in the ground pork and mix well. Divide the mixture into 6 equal portions set on a sheet of waxed paper.

3 Open up the thawed pastry sheets and cut each sheet into thirds. Roll out each piece to form a nice rectangle, about 12 x 4 inches. Lay a portion of the pork filling down the center of each rectangle, and shape the meat into a narrow line down the center of the rectangle, about 1½ inches across and ½ inch tall. Fold the dough over the meat to make a roll—like a long, thin pig in a blanket. Repeat with the remaining pieces of dough and meat filling.

4 Moisten the pastry seams with a small amount water and press to seal. Cut each long roll across into sections about 1½ inches wide. Place the little sausage rolls on the parchment-lined pans, leaving a little over an inch between the rolls.

5 Bake until the pastry is deep golden brown, about 25 minutes.

WADE BENNETT

Rockridge Orchards & Cidery

All farmers are magicians, to some degree. In Wade Bennett's case, picture the talents of Merlin, Gandalf, and Dumbledore all rolled up into one mustachioed, baseball-capped fellow. He's been making an assortment of magical potions at his orchards in Enumclaw for a couple of decades, and the names and flavor profiles of thousands of fruits are filed in his remarkable mental database for seemingly instant recall.

Part of being a magician is being geeky enough to own the label, and Wade clearly enjoys sharing his knowledge. A few years ago, he convinced his wife, Janice, to let him buy one $1,100 oak barrel from France. He used this barrel to age some apple cider vinegar, calling the final product Rocksalmic Vinegar. Its flavor is stupendous—so good that Janice wholeheartedly agreed to up the quantity of those expensive barrels so they'd have more of this special vinegar for future years.

Wade was one of the first guys in the state to apply for a new craft distillery license. Now he has two stills up and running, turning cider into the country's richest apple brandy. It's potent stuff, but the pure depth of apple flavor comes through in every sip, and there's no finer liquid for deglazing a pan of pork chops or stirring into an apple pie filling. One of the stills producing this excellent booze is a fine, upstanding piece of lab equipment; the other has a distinct personality. It's named Fifi, after Wade's French mother-in-law. As Wade says, "They're both beautiful French ruins." Anyone with even a drop of romance in their souls must assume that it's Fifi producing the apple brandy.

A visit to his market stand is always

an education: as the seasons shift, so do the mysteries. Early spring offers tea camellias and yuzu bushes; summer brings fresh shiso leaves; fall is an endless parade of apple and pear varieties. If it's known to be ugly, tricky to grow, and immensely flavorful, chances are you will find it on Wade's tables. There's just as much choice among the ciders. There's a mulled version, and apples blended with raspberries, strawberries, and blueberries. In the category of plain ol' apple cider, you'll find country (a little sweet), tart, and Honeycrisp flavors. There's also Asian pear cider. In the cold months of the year, you can warm up at his stand with a cup of hot cider, and when the weather is warm, you'll find raspberry-apple cider granitas, pure bliss when it's 90 degrees out.

In 2010, Wade added a piece of real estate to his operation that's the tiniest bit more urban than the orchards. The Rockridge Orchards Country Market is very much an indoor farmers' market. Depending on the season, the bins are loaded with produce from the farm, or jams and pastries made by friends, or goods that Wade picks up on the return trip from delivering his cider out to the dry side of the mountains. There's a tasting room, of course, and in 2011 they planted a new orchard around the building, so in a few years they'll be hosting the sort of orchard harvest events that every Washington parent should bring their kid to. See this tree, sweetie? This is where the cup of cider you're drinking came from. And this man here, with the mustache and baseball cap? He's the wizard who made it all happen.

WHITE SALAD WITH GRILLED SARDINES

From Betty Restaurant

Celery is a vegetable that seems like an alien species the first time you buy it from a farmers' market. We've heard conflicting reports as to whether the differences are the result of growing conditions or specific varieties, but Seattle celery is about five shades darker than the standard grocery store stuff. It has a stronger flavor, too, with a fresh, peppery bite. Although this recipe suggests using the inner stalks, you'll notice that they're not particularly pale. During local celery season, it's a Green and White Salad, for sure. The whole point to this plate is the blending of flavors: tangy lemon, unctuous and fruity olive oil, smoky grilled sardines, bright fennel. In order to set off these ingredients properly, you'll want to make sure you've got just the right balance of lemon, oil, and salt—as you dress the greens, taste a few leaves to make sure.

2 SMALL CANS GOOD-QUALITY
   OIL-PACKED SARDINES
6 CUPS FRISÉE
4 CELERY STALKS, PREFERABLY
   TENDER PALE-GREEN STALKS
   FROM THE CENTER, THINLY
   SLICED THIN ON THE DIAGONAL
1 FENNEL BULB, TRIMMED OF
   STALKS AND SHAVED PAPER
   THIN

1 TBSP MINCED SHALLOT
1 LEMON
EXTRA-VIRGIN OLIVE OIL
KOSHER SALT
SHAVED PARMESAN CHEESE FOR
   GARNISH
FRESHLY GROUND BLACK PEPPER

Serves 6
Gluten-free

1 Preheat a very clean gas grill to high. When it's hot, gently remove the sardines from the cans, being careful to keep them whole. Place the sardines on the grill and char them on both sides. Once charred, gently transfer them to a plate and keep warm.

2 Place the frisée, celery, fennel, and shallot in a large bowl. Cut the lemon in half and squeeze a small amount of juice over the mixture. (You can always add more.) Add some olive oil and a generous pinch of salt and toss thoroughly. Taste, and adjust the flavors as needed. This process may be repeated several times until your palate judges it exactly right.

3 Portion the salad in the center of 6 plates, making sure that the various ingredients are equally dispersed. Place the warm sardines on top. Garnish each plate with shaved Parmesan cheese and a little freshly ground black pepper.

Edible Tips

Thanks to a healthy Pacific sardine population, our region's sardines are highly sustainable; unfortunately, most U.S. canneries are a thing of the past. There's a great cannery in California that packs boneless, skinless filets in olive oil on Steinbeck's famous Cannery Row (CanneryRowSardineCo.com).

You don't have to go as far outside our region for olive oil as you might think. The Oregon Olive Mill—owned by the same folks who produce Durant Vineyards wine—planted olive trees early in this century and produce three kinds of olive oil. For this salad, the strong, peppery Koroneiki is a great choice (www.NorthwestWinestoYou.com).

OUEFS PLAT

From Peyrassol Café at Southport

While this dish is lovely for a weekend breakfast—it's easy to assemble while you're brewing your coffee—it makes an exceptionally cozy supper to come home to after work. We like soft egg yolks best, as they make a gorgeously rich sauce for the bread and cheese. Chef Sachia Tinsley urges using cage-free eggs, but we suggest going a step further. When eggs are the central part of a dish, it's important that they be exceptional. If you keep chickens yourself, or have a friend who does, you're set. Alternatively, get to your neighborhood farmers' market early and pick up a dozen eggs laid by birds who run amok on our local polyculture farms, scratching up bugs to supplement their organic grain diets. If these are out of your price range, look for organic free-range eggs with an Animal Welfare Approved label.

Edible Tip

White truffle oil is pricey, but a few drops go a long way and it's certainly less spendy than buying an actual white truffle. La Buona Tavola in Pike Place Market sells bottles of Italian white truffle oil in several sizes, and Oregon Truffle Oil uses the Northwest white truffle for a similar, somewhat lighter, effect (see Resources, page 162).

4 THIN SLICES PROSCIUTTO
   DI PARMA
2–4 TBSP GRATED BEECHER'S
   FLAGSHIP CHEESE (OR ANY
   TANGY, RICH CHEESE WORKS
   NICELY—THINK AGED GOUDA,
   SHARP CHEDDAR, OR SAMISH
   BAY AGED LADYSMITH CHEESE)
4 LARGE EGGS
EXTRA-VIRGIN OLIVE OIL
FRESH GROUND BLACK PEPPER

WHITE TRUFFLE OIL
MACRINA BAKERY POTATO BREAD
   (OR YOUR FAVORITE BAGUETTE-
   STYLE BREAD), BRUSHED
   WITH OLIVE OIL AND LIGHTLY
   TOASTED

Serves 2
Gluten-free (if served with gluten-free bread)

1 Preheat the oven to 350°F. In each of two shallow 5-inch round ovenproof ramekins, place 2 slices of the prosciutto. Divide the grated cheese evenly over the prosciutto. Carefully crack 2 eggs over the cheese in each ramekin, drizzle the yolks with just a touch of olive oil, and place on a baking sheet.

2 Bake for 5 minutes; then rotate the baking sheet and bake for another 3–5 minutes, depending on how set you like your yolks.

3 Using oven mitts, transfer each ramekin to a dinner plate lined with a napkin (to keep the ramekin from sliding around). Sprinkle the eggs with fresh cracked black pepper and finish with a drizzle of white truffle oil. Serve with the toasted potato bread.

CARAMELIZED ONION OVEN PANCAKE

From Anne Catherine Kruger

Anne Catherine Kruger has a special place of honor behind the scenes at Edible Seattle: of the countless recipes we've procured over the years from chefs, fishermen, farmers, and residents of Seattle, she's the only one who's sent us a recipe where every single ingredient listed its source—and every source was found at her nearby farmers' market. What the rest of us might see as astonishing dedication, she sees as a matter of course. This recipe makes a brilliant brunch or late-night supper, as the pancake batter needs a lengthy rest in the fridge. You can also caramelize the onions well in advance—up to a week—and reheat them right before you cook the pancakes. To make several pancakes all at once, we suggest using pie plates rather than sauté pans. Warm up the onions in the microwave, pour on the pancake batter, and cook for an extra 3–5 minutes in the oven.

Edible Tip

For more of a flavor contrast, try the tiniest drizzle of balsamic honey vinegar from Honey Ridge Farms (HoneyRidgeFarms.com). Its bold, sweetly tangy flavor complements the caramelized onions beautifully.

6 LARGE EGGS
1 CUP WHOLE MILK
¼ TSP APPLE CIDER VINEGAR
1 CUP ALL-PURPOSE FLOUR
1 STICK (8 TBSP) UNSALTED BUTTER, MELTED AND COOLED
2 TBSP EXTRA-VIRGIN OLIVE OIL
4 LARGE WHITE ONIONS, VERY THINLY SLICED INTO HALF-MOONS
DASH OF SALT
CLARIFIED BUTTER OR BUTTER/OIL MIXTURE FOR GREASING THE PAN
HEAVY CREAM FOR GARNISH
FRESHLY GROUND BLACK PEPPER

Makes about 4 pancakes
Vegetarian

1 In a large bowl, beat the eggs until the yolks and whites have been well blended. Whisk in the milk and stir in the vinegar. Gently whisk in the flour—it's okay if there are some lumps; it's more important not to overmix. Stir in the butter, again being careful not to overmix. Let the batter rest in the fridge, covered, overnight.

2 In a wide, heavy sauté pan, heat the olive oil over medium-high heat. Add the onions and toss them around in the hot oil to coat. Spread the onions in an even layer across the bottom of the pan and let cook, stirring occasionally, for 10 minutes. Add the salt and continue cooking until the onions are a rich dark brown, about another 20 minutes. Transfer to a small bowl.

3 When you're ready to eat, preheat the oven to 450°F. Heat an oven-safe pan, between 9 and 11 inches in diameter, over medium-high heat until the pan is hot. Brush the pan generously with clarified butter or a blend of butter and a little vegetable oil. Evenly distribute one-quarter of the onions across the bottom of the pan and ladle a thin layer of pancake batter over the onions. Just as the sides begin to puff up a bit, place the pan in the oven until the pancake is puffed and the batter is set and won't sink in the middle when touched with a finger, 8–11 minutes.

4 Turn the hot pancake over onto a plate as soon as it comes out of the oven. After it falls, drizzle with a touch of heavy cream, grind fresh black pepper to taste, and serve immediately.

5 Repeat with the remaining onions and pancake batter.

CASCADE GRANOLA

Nothing makes a kitchen smell more delicious than baking a pan of slow-cooking granola. While granola is infinitely variable, our version keeps it generally local, blending rolled spelt, hazelnuts, and dried cherries for a deeply central Cascades feel. Chukar Cherries provides three no-sugar-added dried-cherry choices: Rainier, Bing, and Montmorency. Think of these options as the Three Bears, with Rainier being almost too sweet for anyone but kids or hummingbirds and the Montmorency verging on too tart for comfort. Bing cherries are just right, hitting the happy medium of complexity and sweetness.

Rolled spelt flakes are thicker than rolled oats, and once they're toasted they have a lovely crunch. They can be substituted in most oatmeal recipes, like cookies or fruit crisp, or cooked up as hot cereal. Lentz Spelt Farm was the first certified organic spelt crop in the state, and you can now find Washington-grown spelt flakes under the Bob's Red Mill label.

Edible Tip

To extend the shelf life of homemade granola, skip stirring in the dried fruit at the end. The toasted mixture of nuts and grains will stay crisp in an airtight container for up to a month. Add a scoop of dried fruit when you're ready to eat.

3 CUPS ROLLED SPELT FLAKES OR OLD-FASHIONED ROLLED OATS
1 CUP CHOPPED BLANCHED HAZELNUTS
1 CUP UNSWEETENED COCONUT FLAKES
¼ CUP FIRMLY PACKED BROWN SUGAR
¾ TSP GROUND CINNAMON
¼ TSP SALT
¼ CUP HONEY
2 TBSP CANOLA OR PEANUT OIL
1 LARGE EGG WHITE
1½ CUPS DRIED CHERRIES, SWEET OR TART VARIETIES

Makes about 6 cups
Vegetarian
Dairy-free
Gluten-free (if made with certified gluten-free oats)

1 Preheat the oven to 300°F. Line a sheet pan with parchment paper and spray with baking spray or lightly coat with vegetable oil.

2 Combine the spelt, hazelnuts, coconut, brown sugar, cinnamon, and salt in a large mixing bowl. In a small pitcher, combine the honey and oil and heat in the microwave for 20–40 seconds, until the honey is warm and easily pourable. Drizzle the liquid into the dry ingredient mixture and toss with a rubber spatula to coat evenly.

3 In a small dish, whisk the egg white until it's white and foamy. Fold this into the granola; you want the grains and nuts to clump up slightly at this point, so don't overmix. Spread the mixture evenly on the prepared sheet pan.

4 Bake for about 50 minutes, taking the pan from the oven to turn the mixture every 10 minutes to ensure even baking. At the 20-minute mark, use a metal spatula to lift and turn sections of the granola to help encourage even browning without breaking up the clusters. At the 40-minute mark, begin checking the color every 5 minutes. The goal is toasted grains that are a rich, crispy brown without a hint of being scorched.

5 At the granola begins to cool down, you can break up any overly large clusters with a spoon. The cooler it gets, the crunchier it will get, so this is most easily done in the first few minutes after baking. Stir in the dried fruit and cool. Store in an airtight container in the pantry or freezer.

SEEDLESS HUCKLEBERRY JELLY

4 CUPS RED HUCKLEBERRIES
1½ CUPS SUGAR
2 TSP FRESH LEMON JUICE

Makes 1½ cups jelly
Vegetarian
Gluten-free

Red huckleberries are tiny and bright crimson red—and if you don't happen to have a bush in your backyard, chances are you can find one pretty easily, since they're a common native species in the lowland forests of Western Washington. Our region's native tribes relied on them for vitamin C. The berry flavor is fresh and tart, similar to a red currant, and the thornless, chest-high bushes make for easy picking. Be sure to leave a few behind for the birds, who love these fruits at least as much as we do. This jelly has a beautiful bright crimson color, and the recipe can easily be scaled up if you're lucky enough to have a large quantity of berries. It will keep in an airtight tub in the fridge for several months and doesn't require special canning procedures. Its tangy flavor is delicious in Jam Oatmeal Streusel Bars (page 154).

1 Rinse and pick over the berries, removing any stray stems. In a medium saucepan, mash the berries with a potato masher or a few spins of an immersion blender. Add 1 cup water and simmer over medium heat until the berries are completely soft, about 10 minutes. Remove from the heat.

2 Pour the cooked berries into a fine-mesh sieve or colander lined with cheesecloth set over a medium bowl. With a large spoon or silicone spatula, press and stir the berries to extract as much juice as possible. You should end up with about 2 cups of juice in the bowl, and a mash of seeds and skins in the strainer (the mash can be composted or thrown away).

3 Pour the juice into a clean medium saucepan and add the sugar and the lemon juice. Add additional sugar according to taste; the chilled jelly will be less sweet than the juice tastes at room temperature. Heat the sweetened juice to a low boil over medium-high heat, stirring continually. Allow the juice to bubble until it becomes slightly thick and concentrated, 10–15 minutes.

4 Cool the mixture completely; then pour into an airtight container. Store the jelly in the fridge.

Edible Tip

Washington allows everyone to pick up to 3 gallons of red huckleberries per year for personal use; be sure to pick on lands in the state trust and not in national parks. You can find more details about when and where to pick at the Department of Natural Resources website (DNR. wa.gov).

Don't have time to pick your own? Northwest Wild Foods sells gallon-size bags of frozen huckleberries, which make fantastic jelly. Use any leftovers for pancakes, pie, or a berry shortcake (see Resources, page 162).

HEIRLOOM APPLE BUTTER

Apple butter is the easiest beginner jam there is—no fussy preparation, no special tools, and, unlike other fruit jams, it's made at the time of year when it feels cozy to have the stove on for several hours at a time. This spiced version can be used for baking (try it in Jam Oatmeal Streusel Bars, page 154) as a condiment for ham or pork chops, or spread on your morning toast. We provide instructions for storing in the freezer or fridge, but this recipe can be home-canned using the boiling-water method (follow your canner's directions).

5 LB APPLES
2 CUPS FRESH APPLE CIDER
2 CUPS SUGAR
JUICE FROM ½ LEMON
1 TSP GROUND CINNAMON
¾ TSP GROUND ALLSPICE

Makes 4 pints
Vegan
Gluten-free

1 Quarter the apples, removing the stems. Combine the apples and cider in a large, heavy pot and simmer, covered, over medium heat until the apples are completely soft, between 30 and 80 minutes, depending on the variety.

2 Run the cooked apples through a food mill or push them through a fine-mesh sieve to remove the seeds and skins.

3 Rinse the pot to remove any leftover apple skins and return the apple pulp to the pot. Add the sugar and lemon juice and cook over low heat for several hours, stirring occasionally, until the mixture is a rich reddish brown and is thick enough to stay mounded up on a spoon or small plate. Stir in the spices.

4 Let the apple butter cool to warm room temperature and ladle into airtight 2-cup storage tubs. Label and freeze for up to 4 months, or store in the fridge for up to 1 month.

Edible Tip

It was Wade Bennett of Rockridge Orchards (see his profile, page 119), who first suggested to us that we replace the more usual water in apple butter with fresh, tart apple cider. It's a great change for two reasons—first, as you might expect, the flavor is that much more intense. The bigger surprise is how much prettier the apple butter ends up being. Maybe it's the color, and maybe it's the extra fructose, but cider provides a glittery sheen and depth of color that water-based apple butter lacks.

Apple butter is a forgiving way to use up an assortment of apple varieties, and seconds—apples with dings, or of a smaller size, or more russeting than first-quality fruits—are an inexpensive option we love. Any blend of sweet or tart apples is fine, as long as you include a few with red skins for their pretty coloration.

CHAPTER 5

DESSERTS AND DRINKS

For being a generally healthy city, Seattle has a surprising nationwide reputation for its sweet tooth. Not that there's anything wrong with ending your meal with a cheese plate, but generally we prefer pie. Or cupcakes. Or ice cream. Or all of the above. These desserts keep it seasonal with Washington's outstanding fruit, and thanks to the astonishing feats of farming on both sides of the mountains, we can even get the flour and butter from within a few hundred miles of home. Dedicated locavores practically have a moral obligation to eat dessert.

As for beverages, we like to embrace those that are equally pleasurable with or without alcohol—it's no fun raising a celebratory glass if half the party is sipping plain seltzer. Here you'll find sophisticated herbal syrups that form the basis for all sorts of deeply northwestern drinks.

EDIBLE SEATTLE'S ALL-BUTTER CRUST

Somewhere in the recent generations, pie became a bugaboo to home cooks, and the fear created a Catch-22, because confidence turns out to be a key ingredient in making a good piecrust. Even if you've had disappointing experiences making piecrusts, we urge you to give it another shot. Since publishing this recipe in the fall of 2008, we've had feedback from all over the country that this recipe works like a charm (our designer even switched to it from her grandmother's old recipe). Pick a day when it's not too hot and you're feeling sassy— and it'll all turn out perfectly. With that one success you'll be forever hooked. The butter-to-flour proportions in this recipe came about for two reasons. First, it makes the dough very easy to roll out, and it won't tear or stick. Second—and most important—it makes enough dough to generously fit a 9-inch pie pan, leaving you plenty of extra for decorative trim or little piecrust cookies. We routinely opt for the latter, spreading on a bit of butter and a heap of cinnamon sugar. These cookies are the only surefire way to keep greedy cooks like ourselves away from the pie before serving time.

1¼ CUPS ALL-PURPOSE FLOUR
¼ TSP SALT
1 STICK (8 TBSP) COLD UNSALTED FARMSTEAD BUTTER, CUT INTO 1-INCH DICE AND CHILLED AGAIN

4–6 TBSP CHILLED WATER

Makes 1 generous 9-inch crust

1 Blend the flour and salt together in a medium bowl. Sprinkle the chilled butter cubes over the flour and press into the dry ingredients with your fingertips, blending them together until the mixture looks like fresh breadcrumbs or damp sand. Ideally, no lumps of butter any bigger than a pea will remain, nor will you have any dry flour lurking in the bottom of the bowl. Add the cold water 1 tablespoon at a time, blending gently with a large fork, until the dough forms into a ball.

2 On a lightly floured work surface, roll the dough out to about ⅛ inch thick. Fold the crust in half and gently fit the pastry into a 9-inch pie pan. Trim the edge with a sharp knife or scissors so the dough hangs over the edge by ½ inch. Fold and crimp the edge. Line with plastic wrap and freeze for a minimum of 30 minutes, or as long as overnight.

3 Remove from the freezer when your filling's ready and the oven is preheated—whatever sort of pie you're baking, you want the crust fully frozen when it goes into the oven for the crispest, flakiest results.

Edible Tips

Good local butter has a high price tag. If your pie filling has robust flavor—like a spicy pumpkin custard—then chances are the buttery crust flavor will be overpowered and expensive butter would be a silly choice. But if you're making a delicate lemon chess or double-crust apple, opt for the best butter you can afford. Golden Glen Creamery makes lovely farmstead butter in the Skagit Valley, and during the summer months you can find the excellent pasture butter from Organic Valley.

A pastry cloth is the most helpful piecrust accessory you can have. Lay it out on your rolling surface, cover heavily with flour, and roll out your crust. Much of the flour will be absorbed, and the crust will neither stick to the cloth nor absorb so much flour that it dries out. You can find the cloths at kitchen stores and many hardware stores, sold with rolling pin covers. The covers get saggy and aren't worth the trouble.

TRUSTWORTHY APPLE PIE

This pie requires the apples to be so tart you wouldn't necessarily eat them out of hand. While we like to use our favorites from local farms, we'll admit to using Granny Smiths if the urge for apple pie strikes after the farmers' market season is over—it's not the same, but it's the closest we've found.

Edible Tip

Kate McDermott of Art of the Pie shared with us a fine bit of wisdom in apple pie preparation: if you're buying farmers' market varieties, the skins tend to be thinner and you don't need to peel the apples. The peels contain tannins, which add to the flavor of the pie. Grocery store apples are nearly all thicker-skinned varieties and are best peeled.

In a good year, market tables are awash in interesting apple varieties. Here's a list of tart apples that hold their shape nicely during cooking, making them perfect choices for pie. (The season starts as early as August and goes through to mid-November.)

- Bramley
- Belle de Boskoop
- Calville Blanc d'Hiver
- Cox Orange Pippin
- Elstar
- Jonagold
- Karmijn de Sonnaville
- King of Tompkins County

2 (9-INCH) PREPARED PIECRUSTS (MADE FROM 2 SEPARATE BATCHES OF EDIBLE SEATTLE'S ALL-BUTTER CRUST; RECIPE FOLLOWS)

8 CUPS TART BAKING APPLES (ABOUT 8 APPLES), CORED AND VERY THINLY SLICED (LEAVE UNPEELED)

½ CUP GRANULATED SUGAR

¼ CUP FIRMLY PACKED DARK BROWN SUGAR

3 TBSP ALL-PURPOSE FLOUR

¼ TSP GROUND CINNAMON

⅛ TSP FRESHLY GRATED NUTMEG

Makes 1 (9-inch) pie
Vegetarian

1 Adjust one oven rack to the lowest possible position in the oven, and leave the other rack in the middle or upper third of the oven. Preheat the oven to 375°F.

2 Fit one of the crusts into a 9-inch pie pan and freeze as directed in the recipe. Roll the second crust out into a 10-inch circle, brush off any excess flour, transfer to a parchment paper–lined baking sheet, cover with plastic wrap, and refrigerate until firm, at least 20 minutes.

3 Place the apple slices in a large bowl. Combine both sugars and the flour, cinnamon, and nutmeg in a small bowl and sprinkle over the apples. Toss until coated (fingers work best) and pour into the bottom crust.

4 Peel the plastic wrap away from the refrigerated pastry sheet, place on top of the filling, and trim to a ¼-inch overhang. Tuck the top edge inside the bottom's crimped edge and cut a few slits in the top for steam to escape.

5 Bake on the lowest rack of the oven for 35 minutes. At that point, move the pie to a higher oven rack and bake until the top is golden brown and the filling is bubbling through the slits, another 25–35 minutes.

6 Transfer to a rack to cool. Serve warm or at room temperature.

FRESH PEACH PIE

From Kate McDermott, Art of the Pie

Kate McDermott's peach pie is unbeatable. Such velvety filling is the ideal expression of a summer fruit pie; it's neither watery nor gelatinous. For her Art of the Pie classes, she brings in Frog Hollow peaches from California, which are Brix tested for ideal sweetness, packed with tender loving care, and shipped up to a local grocery chain for midsummer's Peach-O-Rama. As our northerly farmers devote more attention to this fragile fruit, and as our climate seems to be increasingly better for peach quality, we suggest heading toward some of the smallest fruit stands at our farmers' markets. Rama Farm and Little Wing Farm—each just a couple of acres in central Washington—bring their peaches to market individually wrapped and at the very peak of perfection.

Edible Tip

Quality is more important than varietal when you're choosing peaches. Avoid any hint of green on the skin near the stem—look for undertones of creamy yellow or orange. We appreciate the stands where the farmer chooses for you—the fruit is less bruised if it's not picked over. If you pick your own, choose fruits that are noticeably heavy for their size, and you'll have juicier, sweeter peaches.

2 (9-INCH) PREPARED PIECRUSTS (MADE FROM 2 SEPARATE BATCHES OF *EDIBLE SEATTLE*'S ALL-BUTTER CRUST, PAGE 130)

6 CUPS FRESH PEACHES, CHOPPED INTO COARSE BITE-SIZED CHUNKS

¼–½ CUP SUGAR, ACCORDING TO THE SWEETNESS OF THE FRUIT, PLUS 1 TBSP TO SPRINKLE ON TOP OF THE CRUST

PINCH OF FRESHLY GRATED NUTMEG

⅓ TSP SALT

½ CUP ALL-PURPOSE FLOUR

½–1 TBSP QUICK-COOKING TAPIOCA, IF THE FRUIT IS ESPECIALLY JUICY

½ TBSP BUTTER

1 LARGE EGG WHITE MIXED WITH 1 TBSP WATER

Makes 1 deep-dish 9-inch pie

1 Preheat the oven to 425°F.

2 Fit one of the crusts into a deep-dish 9-inch pie pan and freeze as directed in the recipe. Roll the second crust out into a 10-inch circle, brush off any excess flour, transfer to a parchment paper–lined baking sheet, cover with plastic wrap, and refrigerate until firm, at least 20 minutes.

3 While the pastry is chilling, combine the peaches, ¼–½ cup of the sugar, nutmeg, salt, flour, and tapioca (if needed) in a large mixing bowl. Blend the mixture with your hands until the fruit looks like it is coated with coarse wet sand.

4 Place the filling in the chilled bottom crust. Cut or tear the butter into small pieces and dot the peach filling with them.

5 Peel the plastic wrap away from chilled pastry sheet, place on top of the filling, and trim to a ¼-inch overhang. Tuck the top edge inside the bottom's crimped edge and cut a few slits in the top for steam to escape.

6 Using a pastry brush, paint a small amount of the egg-white wash on top of the pie (you won't need too much) and sprinkle with the remaining 1 tablespoon of sugar.

7 Bake for 15 minutes at 425°F. Reduce the oven temperature to 350°F and bake for another 35–45 minutes. Let rest for at least 30 minutes before serving. This pie is best eaten the same day it's baked, but leftover slices can be kept either in the fridge or at room temperature for another day or two.

HOTT CHERRY ICE CREAM

From Zephyr Paquette

Aside from being such a great ice cream that people reminisce about it 18 months after eating a scoop, we love this recipe for highlighting an unusual local ingredient and for making excellent use of a common one. When sweet cherries are abundant in June, it's simple enough to pit and freeze bags of them—but the texture of a frozen cherry isn't too appealing. Using the juice and tossing out the mushy fruit is a smart choice. Any variety of sweet cherry is fine, be it Rainier, Bing, or a mix of several. Zephyr turned us on to the ground peppers from Some Like It Hott, a Port Townsend–based spice company that grows several kinds of chile in their greenhouses and processes them into ground chili powders with fresh and complex flavors. The Basque pepper used here, piment d' Espelete, is a touch hotter than dried jalapeño and far more interesting. *Note:* The frozen cherries need to meld with the piment d' Espelete and sugar overnight, and the custard needs to freeze for several hours, so plan accordingly.

Edible Tip

Bings are a great choice for the frozen cherries—they're easily available and have a reliable balance between sweet and acidic flavors. Rainier and Queen Anne are the only sweet cherries not recommended—they're so sweet and nonacidic that the caramel loses some of its deliciousness.

FOR THE CHERRY SYRUP:
4 CUPS FROZEN PITTED SWEET CHERRIES
1–3 TSP SOME LIKE IT HOTT SMOKED PIMENT D' ESPELETE, DEPENDING ON YOUR TOLERANCE
½ CUP SUGAR

FOR THE CUSTARD:
4 CUPS HEAVY CREAM
1 CUP WHOLE MILK
1 (14 OZ) CAN SWEETENED CONDENSED MILK
¼ CUP CONFECTIONERS' SUGAR
2 EGGS

Makes 1½ quarts
Vegetarian
Gluten-free (if made with gluten-free confectioners' sugar)

1 Combine the frozen cherries, piment d' Espelette, and sugar in a large bowl, cover, and let sit overnight at room temperature.

2 The next day, drain, pressing the cherries firmly to extract as much juice as possible and reserving the liquid. In a small, heavy saucepan, heat the liquid to a light simmer over medium heat. Slowly reduce the liquid to a thick, caramel-like consistency, 10–15 minutes. Pour the syrup into a small bowl and set aside at room temperature while you make the custard.

3 In a medium, heavy saucepan, combine the cream, milk, condensed milk, and confectioners' sugar. Over medium heat, warm the mixture to a low simmer. While the milk is warming, lightly beat the eggs in a small bowl. When the milk is warm, pour ¼ cup of it into the eggs and whisk until smooth; then pour the tempered eggs into the saucepan with the milk mixture. Cook over medium, stirring continually, until slightly thickened, about 8 minutes. Remove from the heat.

4 Cool the custard for several hours in the refrigerator, and freeze according to the manufacturer's instructions for your ice cream maker.

5 When you judge the freezing process to be very nearly complete, pour the ice cream into a 9 x 13-inch freezer-safe baking pan and drizzle the cherry syrup on top. Use a silicone spatula to gently swirl a cherry ribbon through the ice cream. Place the pan in the freezer and freeze for an additional 30–90 minutes before serving. Any leftovers can be kept in a plastic container in the freezer for up to a week.

HONEY ICE CREAM

This ice cream is all about the honey flavor, with nothing added but a touch of vanilla and a whole lot of creamy texture. Because we have such a glorious range of honey varieties around Puget Sound, you can end up with wildly different results simply by varying the type of honey you choose. We're also seeing more honeys from city beekeepers. If you're not interested in being a connoisseur of single-pollen varieties, we suggest you support your own neighborhood honey shop, like the Ballard Bee Company or Seattle Bee Works. Whatever variety you like best, serve the ice cream with a seasonal sablé cookie (Endless Sablés, page 149). If you're the sort of cook who tastes frequently during the cooking process (and we hope you are), don't panic if you think the honey custard is overpoweringly sweet. Because of how temperature affects flavor, once it's frozen it won't taste nearly as sweet.

2 CUPS WHOLE MILK
1 CUP HEAVY CREAM
1 (4-INCH) VANILLA BEAN, SPLIT
4 LARGE EGGS
⅓ CUP HONEY
3 TBSP SUGAR

Makes 1 quart
Vegetarian
Gluten-free

1 Pour the milk and cream into a medium saucepan. Scrape the seeds from the vanilla bean halves into the milk mixture, and set the pan over medium heat. While the milk warms up, beat the eggs in a 4-cup heatproof pitcher; then whisk in the honey and sugar. Once the milk is at a gentle simmer, remove the pan from the heat, pour ½ cup of the hot milk into the eggs, and whisk to combine.

2 Return the pan to the stove and slowly stir the egg-milk mixture into it. Stir constantly and adjust the temperature as necessary to keep the custard hot but not boiling. Cook until the custard coats the back of a spoon and, using your finger on the back of the spoon, you can make a clear trail through it with your finger, 15–20 minutes. Pour the custard into a fine-mesh strainer set over a small pitcher or bowl and push it through using a silicone spatula to remove any lumps. Place a piece of plastic wrap directly on the surface of the custard to keep a skin from forming. Chill the custard until completely cold, at least several hours or overnight.

3 Freeze the chilled custard according to the manufacturer's instructions for your ice cream maker.

APPLE SORBET

From Erin Preston, Urbane

This is the best apple dessert since apple pie. Juicing the fruit with the skins on allows the tasty tannins in the skins to add their complex flavors to the final sorbet, rendering it into an astonishing mouthful of rich apple goodness. As the sorbet melts in your mouth, you'll get the intense experience of biting into a perfect apple with none of the crunching effort. It's nothing short of miraculous. And if you really want to go over the top, sub in Finn River's *méthode champenoise* hard apple cider for the sparkling wine. As a dessert, this sorbet needs nothing more than some buttery sablés on the side (see page 149 for a basic recipe with a few spiced variations). It can also be a fun base for warm winter cocktails. Fill a mug two-thirds of the way with boiling water; then add a generous scoop of the sorbet and a tot of spiced rum or Tuaca, a vanilla-citrus liqueur.

Edible Tip

Erin usually uses Granny Smith apples for this sorbet, partly because they retain their pretty color longer than heirloom varieties. Pippin varieties are delicious, but the sorbet will be light brown. Other apples with dark red skins will impart a prettier pink color.

1 LB (2 CUPS) SUGAR
3 CUPS TART APPLES
1 TBSP FRESH LEMON JUICE
1 CUP CHAMPAGNE OR OTHER
  SPARKLING WINE

Makes 3 quarts
Vegan
Gluten-free (that is, if the champagne is gluten-free; check the brand)

1 Combine the sugar and 4 cups water in a medium saucepan over medium-high heat. Bring to a boil. Let continue to boil until it forms a thick syrup, about 5 minutes. Pour the syrup into a heatproof pitcher and chill for several hours or overnight.

2 When the sugar syrup is well chilled, run the apples through a juicer with the skins on. Add the lemon juice immediately to slow the oxidation of the fresh juice and help retain its color. Stir the apple juice into the cold sugar syrup. Add the champagne. (You will have much of the bottle of champagne left. We are certain you will put it to good use before it goes flat. Cheers!)

3 Pour the mixture into an ice cream maker and process according to manufacturer's directions.

GINGERED PUMPKIN CUSTARD

From Salish Lodge

These individual-serving-size custards are wonderful topped with fresh whipped cream flavored with a pinch of sugar and freshly grated nutmeg. While canned pumpkin is perfectly fine in this recipe, it's even better with Sugar Hubbard squash from Sherman's Pioneer Farm Produce on Whidbey Island. This heirloom variety is big, blue, and warty on the outside but has a creamier texture and a sweeter, richer flavor than even fresh Sugar Pie pumpkins. We've taken to roasting large quantities when it's in season, keeping the freezer stocked with puree for the whole year. Both its flavor and its texture are shown at their finest in this spicy, rich custard.

Edible Tips

Sherman Farms Sugar Hubbard squash is available in big chunks that roast in about 45 minutes. Once it's cooked, you can puree and use it immediately or freeze it in 1-cup tubs.

For the best ginger flavor, we buy whole dried ginger-root and grate it fresh with a microplane right when we need it. The flavor is altogether better—sweeter, hotter, and more complex—and whole roots will last indefinitely. Look for them in Asian markets (see Resources, page 162), or buy from The Spice House (TheSpiceHouse.com).

2 ⅓ CUPS HEAVY CREAM, PLUS ADDITIONAL FOR GARNISH IF DESIRED
1 VANILLA BEAN, SPLIT
5 LARGE EGG YOLKS
¾ CUP SUGAR
1 ⅓ CUPS UNSWEETENED PUMPKIN PUREE
1 TBSP GROUND GINGER

Serves 6
Vegetarian
Gluten-free

1 Preheat the oven to 300°F. Pour the cream into a heavy medium saucepan and scrape the seeds from the split vanilla bean into the cream. Heat the cream and vanilla over medium-high heat until it just boils.

2 While the cream is heating up, combine the egg yolks and sugar in a medium bowl and mix until smooth. When the cream is just boiling, pour ¼ cup of it into the egg-yolk mixture, and stir well. Pour the tempered egg yolks into the hot cream and blend well. Remove from the heat.

3 Add the pumpkin puree and ginger to the hot custard. Pour the custard through a fine-mesh strainer set over a bowl to remove any lumps, pushing it through using a silicone spatula. Skim off any air bubbles. Fill each ramekin with the custard. Let sit 5 minutes; then skim again for air bubbles.

4 Place the ramekins in a large baking pan. Fill the pan with hot water so it comes halfway up the sides of the ramekins. Cover the pan with aluminum foil, making a "tent" with the foil. Use a paring knife or kitchen shears to cut a 2-inch hole in the center of the foil, which will allow steam to escape. Bake for 45 minutes.

5 Carefully remove the water bath from the oven. Transfer the ramekins to a wire rack and let cool. Serve with the sweetened whipped cream.

PEANUT BUTTER AND JELLY ICE CREAM SANDWICHES

*From Lucy Damkoehler,
Taste Restaurant*

Peanut butter and jelly sandwiches always seemed dessert-like—which probably explains their popularity with the elementary school set. This version turns sticky peanut butter into a tasty cookie bar, and the jelly becomes a sophisticated semifreddo that cooks quickly. It's a lovely dessert for a summertime party and comes together with minimal baking time or hovering over a hot stove. Best of all, you can assemble the sandwiches a week or two in advance; they store beautifully in the freezer.

Since apricot season is shorter than we'd like, you can substitute other summer fruits in the semifreddo. If you like the fruit in jam, chances are you'll like it in this dessert. If there are multiple cooks working together on this, you might run into a minor disagreement about whether the sandwiches should be rectangles or triangles. We suggest some of each—and be thankful you don't have crusts to cut off.

FOR THE PEANUT BUTTER BREAD:
1 STICK (8 TBSP) UNSALTED BUTTER, AT ROOM TEMPERATURE
¾ CUP GRANULATED SUGAR
¾ CUP FIRMLY PACKED BROWN SUGAR
½ CUP CREAMY PEANUT BUTTER [NATURAL]
½ TSP VANILLA EXTRACT
2 LARGE EGGS
1½ CUPS ALL-PURPOSE FLOUR
1¼ TSP BAKING POWDER
¾ TSP KOSHER SALT

FOR THE APRICOT SEMIFREDDO:
2 CUPS CHOPPED PITTED APRICOTS (ABOUT 1 LB)
1 CUP GRANULATED SUGAR
1 TSP ALMOND EXTRACT
1 TBSP FRESH LEMON JUICE
½ CUP WHOLE MILK
1 VANILLA BEAN, SPLIT
6 LARGE EGG YOLKS
1½ CUPS HEAVY CREAM

SPECIAL EQUIPMENT
2 (9 X 13-INCH) BAKING PANS

Makes 24 treats
Vegetarian

Make the peanut butter bread:

1 Preheat the oven to 325°F. Butter a 9 x 13-inch baking pan.

2 In a medium bowl, using a wooden spoon, stir together the butter, both sugars, and the peanut butter and vanilla until creamy. Add the eggs, one at a time, mixing well after each. In a separate bowl, combine the flour, baking powder, and salt. Add this to the butter mixture all at once and stir until it is combined. Pour the batter into the prepared baking pan and bake until golden brown, about 15 minutes. Cool completely in the pan.

Make the apricot semifreddo:

3 Line a 9 x 13-inch baking pan with plastic wrap.

4 In a heavy stainless steel pot over medium-high heat, bring 1 cup of the chopped apricots, ½ cup of the granulated sugar, ½ teaspoon of the almond extract, the lemon juice, and 1 cup water to a boil. Turn the heat down to medium and simmer until the mixture is reduced by half. Remove from the heat. Using an immersion blender or very carefully transferring the mixture to a standing blender, blend until smooth.

It's better to use slightly over-ripe apricots here—look for less-expensive seconds at farmers' markets. Our favorite market stands for apricots are Pipitone Farms (available in many regional markets) and Little Wing Farm, which sells only at the Columbia City Farmers Market. The Riland variety has a lovely color; Harlayne apricots are paler but have an incredibly sweet floral quality.

Peaches, raspberries, or blackberries are all delicious fruits for semifreddo, but you'll need to adjust the amount of sugar, depending on the sweetness of the fruit. Remember that the freezing process will affect how sweet the final product tastes, so it's best to slightly oversweeten the warm custard. Berries can be especially tricky to sweeten, as cooking can bring out their acidity.

5 Return the puree to the pot and add the milk. Scrape the seeds from the vanilla bean halves into the mixture and add the egg yolks and the remaining ½ cup granulated sugar and ½ teaspoon almond extract. Use a large whisk or silicone spatula to stir thoroughly. Cook over medium heat, stirring constantly until thick. Remove from the heat and pour into a fine-mesh strainer set over a bowl. Use a spatula to push it through the strainer to remove any lumps. Place a piece of plastic wrap directly on the surface to keep a skin from forming. Chill completely.

6 When the custard is cold, whip the heavy cream to medium peaks in a chilled medium bowl using an electric mixer. Fold the whipped cream and remaining 1 cup chopped apricots into the custard. Pour into the prepared baking pan and freeze for 8 hours.

7 When ready to assemble the sandwiches, remove the peanut butter bread from its pan and cut into 12 squares. Slice the squares in half horizontally, so you have a top and a bottom. Cut the semifreddo into 12 squares the same size as the squares of peanut butter bread. For each sandwich, place a square of semifreddo on the bottom of the bread, then put the top on. Cut the ice cream sandwich in half, just like mom did with your peanut butter sandwich. Eat immediately, or tuck the sandwiches into large freezer bags. They can be stored in the freezer for up to 2 weeks.

TAYLOR GOLD PEAR COBBLER
WITH GINGER AND CARDAMOM

Taylor Gold pears have none of the grainy texture found in other pears—they're positively velvety, and they make an exceptional winter cobbler. We've found these pears at the Rockridge Orchards stand, but the trees aren't known for big crops so they aren't really catching on in many other orchards. The variety is a natural variation from the Comice, so as a second choice, look for those fat beauties; they're much more common. If you're looking for other options, just know that a creamy texture is more important than the flavor profile. The biscuit topping calls for a bit of masa harina. This is a very finely milled cornmeal (Bob's Red Mill is one of many possible brands) that bakes up quite differently from coarser grinds. The goal here is a slight textural variation, not crunchy little rocks!

Edible Cider Pairing

Look for traditional perry ciders, made from cider pears that are as unpleasant to eat straight as they are pleasant to drink. Tieton Cider Works is certified gluten-free, and Eaglemount Wine & Cider on Port Townsend is a touch sweeter. Finnriver and Snowdrift also offer perrys in limited supply. Eaglemount's ginger apple cider is another fine choice with this cobbler, if you prefer a spicier kick.

FOR THE FILLING:
¼ CUP SUGAR
2 TBSP ALL-PURPOSE FLOUR
½ TSP GROUND CARDAMOM
3–4 TAYLOR GOLD PEARS
    (ABOUT 2 LB), PEELED, CORED,
    AND CUT INTO 1-INCH CHUNKS
¼ CUP FINELY CHOPPED
    CRYSTALLIZED GINGER

FOR THE TOPPING:
½ CUP ALL-PURPOSE FLOUR
¼ CUP MASA HARINA
½ TSP BAKING POWDER
¼ CUP SUGAR
½ TSP GROUND CARDAMOM
¼ TSP SALT
½ STICK (4 TBSP) COLD
    UNSALTED BUTTER,
    CUT INTO TABLESPOONS
2 TBSP HEAVY CREAM
FROZEN YOGURT OR ICE CREAM,
    FOR SERVING

Serves 4
Vegetarian

1 Preheat the oven to 350°F. Grease an 8-inch square pan with butter.

Make the filling:

2 In a medium bowl, whisk the sugar, flour, and cardamom to blend. Add the pears and ginger and stir until combined. Transfer to the baking dish.

Make the topping:

3 In another medium bowl, whisk the flour, masa harina, baking powder, sugar, cardamom, and salt together. Add the butter and, using your fingertips or a pastry cutter, work the butter into the dry ingredients until you have pea-size pieces. Add the cream and stir the mixture with a wooden spoon or a fork until it forms a loose dough.

Assemble and bake the cobbler:

4 Using your hands, break walnut-size chunks of the topping dough off and scatter them on top of the filling—the dough will look jagged and won't completely cover the fruit. Bake until the filling is bubbling and the topping is lightly browned, 40–45 minutes.

5 Transfer the pan to a rack to cool for 10 minutes. Serve warm with yogurt or ice cream.

GOTHBERG FARMS CHÈVRE TART

From Shawnna Poynter, Skagit Valley College Culinary Arts & Hospitality Management Program

It's certainly possible to make this tart with a pound of any great chèvre, but you really should try it with some of Rhonda Gothberg's goat cheese, particularly in early spring, when it's made with the richest, creamiest milk of the year. Rhonda's LaMancha does are kept at a distance from the rams, which (thanks to an interesting pheromone change in the does) leads to a less "goaty" cheese flavor than is typical. We think the lightly tangy filling is especially terrific with fresh apricots (or even drizzled with homemade apricot jam), but your guests certainly won't complain if you serve it alongside a big bowl of Alm Hill raspberries or even our inescapable backyard blackberries.

FOR THE FILLING:
1 LB GOTHBERG FARMS CHÈVRE
1 CUP SUGAR
2 TBSP CORNSTARCH
GRATED ZEST OF 1 LEMON
1 TSP VANILLA EXTRACT
2 LARGE EGGS
4 LARGE EGG YOLKS
⅓ CUP SOUR CREAM

FOR THE CRUST:
2 STICKS (16 TBSP) UNSALTED BUTTER, SOFTENED
⅓ CUP SUGAR
PINCH OF SALT
GRATED ZEST OF 1 LEMON
3 LARGE EGGS
1½ CUPS PASTRY FLOUR
⅓ CUP GROUND PINE NUTS

Makes 1 (11-inch) tart
Vegetarian

Make the filling:

1 Bring all the filling ingredients to room temperature. In a large bowl, using an electric mixer, beat together the chèvre and sugar. Beat in the cornstarch, lemon zest, and vanilla. In a medium bowl, beat the whole eggs, egg yolks, and sour cream together until smooth. Beat this mixture into the chèvre mixture in the larger bowl. Cover and set aside while you make the crust.

Make the crust:

2 In a large bowl, combine the butter, sugar, salt, and lemon zest. Beat in the eggs, one at a time. Stir in the flour and ground pine nuts and mix until smooth. Push the dough into a ball, wrap it in plastic wrap, and whack the ball with your hand to flatten it into a thick disk. Chill for 30 minutes.

3 Preheat the oven to 350°F. Unwrap the dough and roll it out on a lightly floured work surface into a 13-inch circle to fit an 11-inch tart pan. Prick it all over with a fork. Bake the crust until light golden brown, about 10 minutes.

4 Remove the crust from the oven, but leave the oven on. Pour the filling into the hot crust and bake for an additional 15–20 minutes, until the custard is just set.

5 Cool on a wire rack and serve with fresh seasonal fruit.

RHONDA GOTHBERG

Gothberg Farms

Rhonda Gothberg's goat's milk cheeses are like the most delicate butter you can imagine. Even the aged varieties have a creamy softness that makes you keep tasting them until, without really noticing, you have sampled a half pound of cheese in one sitting. This blend of luxurious richness and featherweight flavor makes for some of the most compelling cheese in our very cheese-rich region.

The fresh chèvre is the goat cheese that people are most familiar with, and Rhonda's is superb—a little less tangy than most, with much less of the "goaty" flavor that makes chèvre unappealing to some. She explains that those flavors relate to a specific hormonal reaction in the does when the guys are around. She segregates the sexes in her herd, and the milk has a milder flavor as a result. The milk from her LaMancha goats has a higher butterfat content than that of many other breeds, and you can definitely taste that richness. The breed also has a physical feature—a "gopher ear"—that has absolutely nothing to do with their milk quality but makes them look much more adorably alert than your average goat.

As with so many Washington farmstead producers, Rhonda relied on Washington State University classes to provide the basic instruction—in her case, a short cheese-making course followed by livestock adviser training. In the years since, she makes a point of helping new cheese makers get started, and speaking on best practices; she says she's helped dozens of new producers get started.

Gothberg Farms cheeses are easier to find in Bellingham than in Seattle, but Metropolitan Market carries several, and Ray's Boathouse features it on occasion. In 2010, Rhonda did a special promotion with Grand Central Bakery that resulted in a brush with fame: when President Obama came to town, he ordered a salad topped with her feta. This obstetrics nurse-turned-cheese maker from the tiny town of Beaumont, Texas, is deeply proud to have contributed to that lunch.

The eternally fun thing about discovering a talented food artisan is the pleasure of deciding which of their products you like best. The feta? Well, it's less salty than most, and in the spring it's especially rich—it inspires immediate thoughts of souvlaki and salad simply in order to have a whole meal that revolves around it. The gouda? Utterly unlike a sharp cow's milk gouda—like Rhonda's goat's milk cheddar, it would make an exceptional grilled cheese sandwich. The one with nettles mixed in inspires a 15-minute conversation about what nettles taste like. Aside from the obvious "they taste like nettles," the conclusion is that it's green and springlike and grassy, without being sharp or herbal. Whatever you call it, it's lovely. Not that the unseasoned cheeses are boring—not at all—but there's an herb-crusted Deliziadella Tavola (Delight of the Table) that's lush and summery, like a trip to Provence without the TSA hassles, and then there's the big finish, two newer offerings: the just-right-from-a-Texan-cheese maker chile-infused Cinco de Mayo and the Woman of LaMancha, a manchengo style that's been oiled and rubbed with smoked paprika. This last one is a little mysterious, with subtle heat and smoke flavor coming in gently at the end, and with its rich red color, it's the stone fox of the cheese plate. The other cheeses probably whisper about it behind its back—nothing so lovely could possibly be virtuous.

Unlike the cheese maker herself, who is lovely, virtuous, and in possession of a rare talent.

SALTED CARAMEL TART

*From Heather Earnhardt,
Volunteer Park Café*

This tart is the sort of dessert that gets gobbled down by a crowd of people who, moments before, were insisting they were too full to eat another bite. The only mildly tricky part is making the caramel—but don't let it intimidate you if you haven't made it before. The good news is that you'll end up with twice the amount of caramel you need, and it keeps well in the fridge. All you'll need is an excuse for making a second tart.

You might be tempted to serve this tart with whipped cream, but try to resist that urge. Served plain, the textural combination of crunchy and creamy, as well as the flavor combination of sweet and salty, is absurdly delicious. Sometimes lilies really shouldn't be gilded.

FOR THE CRUST:

1 (9 OZ) BOX NABISCO FAMOUS
   CHOCOLATE WAFERS
1 STICK (8 TBSP) UNSALTED
   BUTTER, MELTED

FOR THE CARAMEL:

2 CUPS SUGAR
1 CUP FILTERED WATER
1 CUP HEAVY CREAM
1 STICK (8 TBSP) CHILLED
   UNSALTED BUTTER,
   CUT INTO SMALL PIECES
1 TSP PINK HAWAIIAN ALAEA
   SEA SALT, SMOKED GRAY SALT,
   OR FLEUR DE SEL

FOR THE CHOCOLATE GANACHE:

8 OZ BEST-QUALITY BITTERSWEET
   CHOCOLATE, CHOPPED
   (YOU CAN ALSO USE CHIPS)
1 CUP HEAVY CREAM

Makes 1 (9-inch) tart
Vegetarian

Make the crust:

1 Preheat the oven to 325°F. Grind the cookies in a food processor into crumbs. Drizzle the melted butter over the ground cookies, pulsing to combine. Press the mixture into a 9-inch fluted tart pan. Bake until the crust becomes fragrant, 10–15 minutes. Cool to room temperature.

Make the caramel:

2 In a heavy medium saucepan, bring the sugar and water to a boil over medium-high heat. Do not stir. Brush down the sides of the pan every 5 minutes with a pastry brush dipped in water (this will keep sugar crystals from forming). Continue cooking until the caramel is a dark golden brown, keeping a watchful eye so it doesn't burn. Remove the pan from the heat and slowly pour in the heavy cream, whisking constantly. The hot caramel will bubble up, so be careful. Whisk in the chilled butter pieces. Add the sea salt and whisk to combine. Pour half the caramel into the cooled chocolate crust. Chill until firm, at least 1 hour.

Store the remaining caramel in the refrigerator for your next tart. It also makes a tasty ice cream topping. It keeps nicely for up to 1 month.

In addition to their different colors, the salts suggested for use in this recipe (see Resources, page 162) contain slightly different mixes of trace minerals and vary a bit in the shape of their grains, these differences combining to offer subtly different taste experiences. Do not substitute regular table salt or kosher salt in this recipe; their grain sizes won't work correctly and you'll have either an undersalted or oversalted tart on your hands.

Make the ganache:

3 Place the chocolate in a heatproof medium bowl. Over medium heat, bring the cream to a simmer in a small heavy saucepan. Immediately remove from the heat and pour over the chocolate, stirring with a silicone spatula until the mixture is smooth and glossy.

4 Gently pour the chocolate ganache over the firm caramel, spreading it with an offset spatula. Chill until firm, at least 1 hour. When slicing, use a warm knife (hold it under hot water, then dry before cutting) and wipe the blade off between cuts. Sprinkle each slice with more sea salt, and serve immediately.

CHOCOLATE MACARONS
WITH CHOCOLATE PRALINE CREAM

From Sara Naftaly, Le Gourmand

These classic Parisian cookies have an incredibly delicate texture that only intensifies the rich chocolate flavor. Sara (who shares the kitchen at Le Gourmand with her husband, Bruce; see profile, page 49) suggests using a dark chocolate that's at least 66% pure cacao, and we've been tremendously pleased with several bars from organic, fair trade Theo Chocolate, based in Fremont. Any of the Theo bars between 70% and 80% work beautifully; you can choose single-origin bars, a classic Theo blend, or a bar that supports the Jane Goodall Institute's conservation work. This recipe takes a bit more work than most cookies, but each of the four steps is relatively simple and the glamorous result will be more than worth the effort. Parisian-style macarons are said by some to taste better and have a nicer texture after a couple of days in the fridge, so they're perfect to make ahead of time for a party.

FOR THE MACARONS:
10.5 OZ FINELY GROUND
    ALMOND MEAL
1 (16 OZ) BOX CONFECTIONERS'
    SUGAR
3–4 TBSP DUTCH PROCESS
    COCOA POWDER
7 LARGE EGG WHITES,
    AT ROOM TEMPERATURE
1 TSP FRESH LEMON JUICE
PINCH OF SALT
2 OZ (¼ CUP) FINE SUGAR

FOR THE VANILLA PASTRY
CREAM:
5 LARGE EGG YOLKS
½ CUP GRANULATED SUGAR

2 TBSP ALL-PURPOSE FLOUR
PINCH OF SALT
2 CUPS WHOLE MILK
½ TSP VANILLA EXTRACT

FOR THE CHOCOLATE PRALINE
CREAM:
1¾ CUPS FINE SUGAR
1 CUP ROASTED AND SKINNED
    HAZELNUTS (SEE EDIBLE TIP
    ON PAGE 149)
14 OZ BITTERSWEET DARK
    CHOCOLATE (USE HIGH-QUALITY
    CHOCOLATE WITH AT LEAST
    66% CACAO), CHOPPED
PINCH OF SALT

Makes 4–5 dozen macarons

1 Preheat the oven to 325°F. Line 2 baking sheets with silicone baking mats or parchment paper. In succession, sift the almond meal, confectioners' sugar, and cocoa into a medium bowl; then stir to combine.

2 In a large bowl using an electric mixer, whip the egg whites, lemon juice, and salt together until the whites begin to become opaque. With the mixer on high, add the sugar in a gentle stream and whip until the mixture forms stiff (but not dry or grainy) peaks, about 2 minutes. Using a silicone spatula, fold the almond meal mixture into the egg whites in 4 small additions.

3 Using a pastry bag fitted with a ¼-inch plain tip, pipe the macaron batter into slightly domed rounds of about 1½ inches onto the lined baking sheets, leaving an inch between them for spread. Let them sit at room temperature for 10 minutes; then bake for 20 minutes. They should develop a little dome on top and what is referred to as a "foot" on the bottom.

4 Remove from the oven and let cool completely on the baking sheets. Once they're cool, peel the mat from the bottom of the macarons, not the other way around.

5 In a medium bowl, beat the egg yolks together with ¼ cup of the granulated sugar, the flour, and the salt. Set aside.

6 In a heavy medium saucepan over medium heat, combine the milk, the remaining ¼ cup granulated sugar, and the vanilla. Just as the milk begins to boil, very slowly pour about half the hot milk into the egg yolk mixture, whisking the entire time. Return the saucepan to the heat, and pour the heated egg yolks into the pan. Continue gently whisking as the pastry cream heats, making sure to reach all of the corners of the pan when you stir. Bring the mixture to a boil and cook for about 1 minute, whisking constantly.

7 Remove from the heat and pour into a fine-mesh strainer set over a bowl. With a silicone spatula, push the cream through the sieve to remove any lumps. Lay a piece of plastic wrap directly on the surface of the pastry cream to prevent a skin from forming. Chill completely before using; this will keep in the fridge for several days.

8 Lightly coat a baking pan with vegetable oil. In a heavy-bottomed saucepan over medium heat, make a dry caramel by adding the fine sugar to the pan about a tablespoon at a time, until the sugar melts and turns a lovely amber brown. Use a wooden spoon to gently mix the caramel if it is coloring unevenly. (Be careful not to splash yourself, as hot caramel can burn quite badly.) Remove the pan from the heat and quickly stir in the roasted hazelnuts before the caramel begins to cool.

9 Pour the praline onto the prepared baking sheet. Let cool completely, until it is hard to the touch; then break it into small pieces (use a hammer or a sturdy oyster knife). Put the pieces in a food processor fitted with a blade attachment. Pulse until you have a fine powder. Cover the praline mixture to keep it from getting sticky.

10 Melt the chocolate in the top of a double boiler set over very gently simmering water, stirring until it is smooth. Remove it from the heat and stir in 2 cups of the cold pastry cream. Add half of the praline powder and stir until well combined. Place a piece of plastic directly on the surface and chill until cold again. Add as much of the remaining praline powder as suits your taste, as well as the salt.

11 Put the cold chocolate praline cream in a pastry bag fitted with a large tip, either plain or fluted. Turn a macaron upside down and pipe about ¾ inch of cream on the flat bottom, leaving a little space around the outside edge for overspill. Place the flat base of another macaron on top of the cream. Repeat until all the macarons are filled.

12 Store in airtight containers in the fridge for up to 5 days.

JOE WHINNEY

Theo Chocolate

If you set out to talk chocolate with Joe Whinney, you will end up talking about deforestation, capitalism, and giant snakes before getting around to the products produced by Theo Chocolate. This seems appropriate for a "bean-to-bar" chocolate company: we don't discuss the bar until we cover the bean. And we can't talk about that critically important bean without covering deforestation, capitalism, and, thanks to a long ago run-in between Joe and an enormous reptile, the giant snake.

Joe's originally from Philadelphia (the accent is inescapable, especially if you can get him to say "organic orange"), but like all good transplants, he's crazy about Seattle, and the big brick factory is a physical sign that he's planting roots on this coast. Chocolate came into his life in the midnineties, when he was volunteering for the International Tropical Conservation Foundation and got sent to harvest cacao with a couple of guys. Joe's job was to pick up the harvested pods and defend the party from any potentially deadly snakes. The snake appeared on schedule and was summarily dealt with, and Joe was rewarded with a bite that changed the world. He was handed a cacao pod and instructed to crack the seeds and eat the goopy innards. This sweet mouthful taught him where chocolate actually comes from—a place that involves great natural beauty, terrific people, and more than a little adventure.

Just as Joe had to learn that chocolate didn't spring fully formed from the inside of a plastic wrapper, many of the cacao farmers Theo works with have never had the opportunity to taste a chocolate bar. When Theo gets directly involved with a production area—Tanzania is an ongoing technical project—having the farmers taste the candy is part of the education process.

In Tanzania, it tends to rain heavily at cacao harvest, and instead of drying correctly, the beans get moldy. A group of farmers is working to change that, with Theo's support, by building enclosed boxes where many small farms can ferment and dry their beans together. Quality is increasing thanks to these improvements, and if the effort continues to pay off, Theo might someday offer a Tanzania single-origin bar.

Third-party certification for consumer labels—like Fair Trade—is a big deal for Joe; he says that if chocolate isn't certified Fair Trade, there's a substantially higher chance of abuse at some point in the supply chain. There's a huge temptation for large corporations to greenwash commodities, and official certification from noncompany sources decidedly lessens the chance of error.

The first line that Theo launched was a highly original series of chocolate bars—a blend of fig, fennel, and almond mixed into dark chocolate, or milk chocolate combined with coconut curry. More basic flavors—mint, orange, salted almond—have joined the roster more recently, along with unflavored bars in 45%, 70%, and 85% cacao. Visiting the Theo headquarters, you'll see heaps of samples of these bars to taste on every table, but, more interesting, you'll find new products and limited-edition treats. A late-winter sampling of these treats included apple cider and ginger rose caramels; ganaches flavored with jasmine tea, single-malt scotch, and burnt sugar; a bar of dark chocolate infused with ghost chile; and a white chocolate bar with chopped pistachios. You can also buy cacao nibs and chipotle-spice sipping chocolate. For chocolate lovers, there is no better smell on earth than this shop.

ENDLESS SABLÉS

There is no cookie recipe that's easier or more versatile than a sablé—a French shortbread cookie that's found in some form on just about every dessert menu in town. Ethan Stowell adds cardamom; Erin Preston flavors hers with orange zest and thyme. You can tweak them through the seasons, adding fresh lemon thyme in the spring, anise hyssop in the summer, hazelnuts in the fall, and baking spices or cacao nibs in the winter. Nobody will complain about an unflavored sablé, either, especially if you splurge on some great farmstead butter from Golden Glen Creamery. A few of our favorite variations follow the basic formula, but we encourage you to tweak the flavorings according to what you've got growing in your own garden or your personal mix of favorite spices.

1¼ CUPS ALL-PURPOSE FLOUR
¼ TSP SALT
1 STICK (8 TBSP) UNSALTED
    BUTTER, AT ROOM TEMPERATURE
⅓ CUP CONFECTIONERS' SUGAR

1 LARGE EGG YOLK
¼ CUP GRANULATED OR DEMERARA
    SUGAR, FOR ROLLING

Makes about 4 dozen cookies

1 In a small bowl, whisk together the flour and salt. In a medium bowl using an electric mixer, beat the butter until it's smooth and creamy. Add the confectioners' sugar and beat on medium speed for 1 minute. Add the egg yolk and beat until thoroughly combined. Add the flour mixture in two batches, mixing well after each addition.

2 Put the dough on a large piece of plastic wrap or parchment paper. Shape the dough into a log about 1½ inches in diameter. Place in the fridge for at least 1 hour and up to 2 days.

3 Preheat the oven to 350°F. Line 2 baking sheets with parchment paper.

4 Roll the dough log in granulated or demerara sugar, and slice into disks about ¼ inch thick. Place the disks on the parchment-lined sheets about 1 inch apart. Bake until the edges are golden brown, 15–20 minutes.

5 Transfer the parchment sheets to wire racks and let cool. Store the cookies in an airtight container at room temperature for up to a week.

Edible Tip

For herbal sablés: Just before adding the flour, stir in 2 heaping teaspoons of any minced fresh herb. Anise hyssop, lemon balm, lemon verbena, pineapple sage, orange mint, and any scented geranium are all good choices.

For nutty sablés: After incorporating the flour, stir in ½ cup finely chopped toasted nuts. Hazelnuts, chestnuts, and English and black walnuts are all grown locally.

For spicy sablés: When you're beating the sugar into the butter, add any one of these spices in the given amount: 1 teaspoon freshly ground cardamom, ¾ teaspoon ground cinnamon, ½ teaspoon ground mace, or ½ teaspoon finely ground black pepper.

HOLMQUIST HAZELNUT-APRICOT COOKIES

*From Karra Wise,
Columbia City Bakery*

Holmquist hazelnuts share a minimal resemblance to any other hazelnut. They're lumpy and oblong, with pretty tiger stripes—like the blessed love child of an almond and a pistachio. They have none of the typical bitterness associated with hazelnuts (you don't have to remove their skins, like you typically do with hazelnuts), but rather a raspberry-like bright sweetness that is nothing short of astonishing. The Holmquist orchards (up by the Canadian border in Lynden) grow the rare and delicious DuChilly hazelnut, a nut that is hard to find elsewhere because the odd shape doesn't work with typical processing equipment, and because, sadly, the trees are highly susceptible to filbert blight. Its flavor is so delicious that it's tempting to invest in redesigning the equipment while creating a "cure the blight" research nonprofit. For the dried apricots, look for ones labeled Mediterranean or Turkish. They'll be soft, golden ovals with a sweet flavor. California apricots have a decidedly tart flavor and a tougher, dryer texture that, while tasty in plenty of recipes, doesn't work well in this cookie.

2 ¾ CUPS ALL-PURPOSE FLOUR
¼ TSP CINNAMON
2 TSP GROUND CLOVES
½ TSP BAKING POWDER
4 LARGE EGGS, AT ROOM
  TEMPERATURE
2½ CUPS GRANULATED SUGAR

1 CUP FINELY GROUND
  HOLMQUIST HAZELNUTS
½ CUP SLICED DRIED
  MEDITERRANEAN APRICOTS
1 CUP CONFECTIONERS' SUGAR

Makes about 4 dozen
Vegetarian

1 Sift the flour, cinnamon, cloves, and baking powder together in a medium bowl. In a large bowl using an electric mixer, beat the eggs and granulated sugar together until the mixture is thick and pale yellow. Switch to the paddle attachment or a heavier beater, and add the flour mixture, nuts, and sliced apricots.

2 For a simple icebox cookie, shape the dough into a short log with a 3-inch diameter. Wrap in plastic wrap and refrigerate for 1 hour. For cookies that are rolled out and cut with cookie cutters, roll the dough into a sheet ¼ inch thick on a parchment paper–covered baking sheet. Chill the sheet for 1 hour.

3 Preheat the oven to 325°F. Line a baking sheet with parchment paper. For the icebox-cookie option, remove the log from the refrigerator and cut across into ¼-inch-thick rounds. Set them 2 inches apart on the lined baking sheet. For the rolled-cookie option, remove the dough sheet from the fridge, cut the dough with plain or fluted 3-inch round cutters, and transfer to the baking sheet.

4 Whichever method you choose, bake until the cookies are firm and set, but not yet browning on the edges, 13–15 minutes.

Edible Tip

If you don't use Holmquist hazelnuts, you'll need to first roast and then skin the hazelnuts you do use, as other hazelnut varieties tend to have bitter skins. Toast them in a single layer on a baking sheet in a 300°F oven until you can see the skins curling up and flaking off. While they're still warm, pour them into a clean kitchen towel and rub the skins off.

5 While the cookies are baking, make a glaze by combining the confectioners' sugar and 2 teaspoons water in a small bowl. Add more water as necessary to make a glaze with a very thin consistency.

6 When the cookies are baked, transfer them to a wire rack and immediately brush the glaze on them. As the cookies cool, the glaze will become thin and crackly. Stored in an airtight container at room temperature, these cookies will keep nicely for up to a week.

DESSERTS AND DRINKS

151

HARVEST CAKE WITH CIDER-CINNAMON CREAM CHEESE FROSTING

From Jess Thomson

As a general rule, we don't set out to put vegetables into our sweets. But since Jess dreamed up this cake for us in 2008, it's been our most popular recipe. And for good reason: it's a moist, spicy treat similar to carrot cake, but it contains three late-summer vegetables, a fruit, and a scoop of whole grains. All the vegetables and the whole wheat flour can be picked up from Nash's produce stands; they sell through several farmers' markets, and their freshly ground flour is simply beautiful. Unfrosted and wrapped tightly in plastic, this cake freezes well for up to a month. Baked in a muffin pan instead of the cake pan, you'll end up with 6 fat breakfast muffins or (with the frosting) 6 gorgeous, and magically nutritious, cupcakes.

Edible Tips

If you've got a food processor, the grating blade makes short work of grating all the vegetables and the apple.

Whole wheat flour can be made from white or red varieties of wheat, but most often what you'll find is from red, which has the typical strong, slightly sour whole wheat flavor. White wheat is milder and far less sour, and it's a great way to start introducing whole-grain flour into your baked goods without changing their flavor (see Resources, page 162).

FOR THE CAKE:
1¼ CUPS ALL-PURPOSE FLOUR
½ CUP WHOLE WHEAT FLOUR
1½ TSP BAKING SODA
¾ TSP SALT
¾ TSP GROUND CINNAMON
½ TSP GROUND GINGER
3 LARGE EGGS
1 CUP GRANULATED SUGAR
¼ CUP FIRMLY PACKED BROWN SUGAR
1 TSP VANILLA EXTRACT
½ CUP CANOLA OIL
2 LARGE CARROTS, GRATED (1½ CUPS)
1 LARGE PARSNIP, GRATED (1 CUP)
1 MEDIUM ZUCCHINI, CORED AND GRATED (1¼ CUPS)

1 TART APPLE, CORED AND GRATED (1 CUP)

FOR THE CIDER-CINNAMON CREAM CHEESE FROSTING:
½ STICK (4 TBSP) UNSALTED BUTTER, AT ROOM TEMPERATURE
1 (8 OZ) PACKAGE CREAM CHEESE, AT ROOM TEMPERATURE
2 CUPS CONFECTIONERS' SUGAR
2 TBSP APPLE CIDER
¼ TSP GROUND CINNAMON

Serves 8
Vegetarian
Dairy-free (without the frosting)

1 Preheat the oven to 350°F. Butter a 9-inch square baking pan, line with parchment paper, and butter the paper.

2 Whisk both flours and the baking soda, salt, cinnamon, and ginger together in a medium bowl. In a large bowl, whisk the eggs and both sugars together until very well blended. Add the vanilla and oil, and whisk until completely combined. Using a wooden spoon, stir the egg mixture into the flour mixture; then fold in the grated vegetables and apple, stirring until they're completely coated with batter. Spread the batter evenly into the prepared pan.

3 Bake until a toothpick inserted in the center comes out clean, 45–55 minutes. Let cool for 15 minutes; then invert the cake onto a wire rack. Remove the paper and invert again onto a serving plate. Cool at least 1 hour more.

4 In a food processor fitted with the paddle attachment, whip the butter and cream cheese together on medium speed until light and smooth, about 3 minutes. With the machine on low, add the confectioners' sugar a little at a time, then the cider and cinnamon. Scrape down the side of the bowl, increase speed to high, and whip for 2 minutes. Spread half the frosting on the cooled cake and reserve the other half for another use.

CARAMEL APPLE CIDER CUPCAKES

*Adapted from a recipe
by Cupcake Royale*

Official dessert trends may come and go, but we've been baking cupcakes for the last 20 years and expect to continue doing so for the next 20. We're especially fond of Cupcake Royale for going to such effort in sourcing their ingredients locally—thanks to their butter, milk, eggs, and flour, all their cupcakes are at least 66% native Washingtonian. Some of their seasonal varieties make use of cherries, apples, carrots, or strawberries. This particular combination is an attempt to duplicate the flavors of hot mulled cider, finishing off the spicy, citrusy, apple-spiked goodness with an intense brown sugar frosting. If you or your loved ones are lucky enough to have a fall birthday, look no further for a recipe that pleases kids and adults alike.

Edible Cider Pairing

For a festive adult option, go with a bubbly *méthode champenoise* from either Finn River or Alpenfire Cider. For a party-size volume of a nonalcoholic variety, look for Skagit Fresh Natural Beverages cider at local grocers.

FOR THE CUPCAKES:

3 CUPS ALL-PURPOSE FLOUR
1 TBSP BAKING POWDER
½ TSP SALT
1½ TSP GROUND CINNAMON
¼ TSP GROUND CLOVES
¼ TSP GROUND GINGER
¼ TSP GROUND ALLSPICE
2 STICKS (16 TBSP) UNSALTED
    BUTTER, AT ROOM TEMPERATURE
2 CUPS GRANULATED SUGAR
4 LARGE EGGS
½ TSP VANILLA EXTRACT
GRATED ZEST OF 1 SMALL ORANGE
    (ABOUT 2 HEAPING TSP)
1 CUP WHOLE MILK

1 SWEET BAKING APPLE, PEELED,
    CORED, AND FINELY DICED

FOR THE FROSTING:

2 STICKS (16 TBSP) UNSALTED
    BUTTER
1 CUP FIRMLY PACKED DARK
    BROWN SUGAR
¼ TSP VANILLA EXTRACT
¼ TSP SALT
½ CUP WHOLE MILK
1 (3 OZ) PACKAGE CREAM CHEESE,
    AT ROOM TEMPERATURE
4 ½ CUPS CONFECTIONERS' SUGAR

Makes 24 cupcakes

1 Preheat the oven to 350°F. Line 2 (12-cup) muffin pans with paper liners.

2 In a medium bowl, whisk together the flour, baking powder, salt, and spices. In a large bowl using an electric mixer, beat the butter and granulated sugar together until pale yellow and fluffy, about 2 minutes. Add the eggs one at a time, beating thoroughly after each addition. Add the vanilla and orange zest, beating until just blended. Add one-third of the flour-spice mixture and beat until fully incorporated. Add half the milk and mix to combine. Repeat the procedure until the flour mixture and milk are blended in. Using a silicone spatula, gently fold in the diced apple.

3 Spoon the batter into the muffin tins, filling each cup three quarters of the way full for traditional cupcakes, or very close to the top to get the Cupcake Royale look. Bake until the tops spring back firmly when touched, 20–25 minutes. Cool completely.

4 In a small saucepan over medium heat, melt the butter and brown sugar together until the sugar is dissolved. Stir in the vanilla and salt. Remove from the heat and stir in the milk. Cool to room temperature. Using an electric mixer, beat in the cream cheese until fully incorporated; then add the confectioners' sugar about ½ cup at a time, until the frosting is thick and smooth. When the cupcakes are cooled completely, frost them.

JAM OATMEAL STREUSEL BARS

From Jess Thomson

Jess Thomson originally developed this recipe to make use of leftover cranberry sauce at Thanksgiving—and we still agree that the combination of tart sauce and sweet brown sugar is tasty. But for most of us, cranberry sauce is around the house just once or twice a year, and these rich, quick cookies are fantastic all year round. The streusel is sweet enough that a less sweet jam (sour cherry, red huckleberry, or high-quality raspberry or blackberry) Makes for the most pleasing flavor contrast, but homemade apple butter (Heirloom Apple Butter, page 127) comes in a close second. Or, if you ever find your fridge overrun with half-empty jam jars, just swirl them all together and call it "summer fruit." In our experience, people will assume this means "highfalutin gourmet" and not ask further questions.

Edible Tip

These bars are one of those treats that are equally good right out of the oven or after sitting on the counter for a day or two. Fresh, the cookie provides a crumbly counterpoint to the filling, and they're a bit messy to eat. After 24 hours, the layers meld more tightly and are easier for kids to eat with their hands. Covered, they can be stored in the fridge or at room temperature for up to a week.

FOR THE CRUST:
2 ¼ CUPS ALL-PURPOSE FLOUR
⅓ CUP FIRMLY PACKED BROWN SUGAR
¼ TSP SALT
2 STICKS (16 TBSP) COLD UNSALTED BUTTER, CUT INTO ½-INCH PIECES
1 CUP OLD-FASHIONED ROLLED OATS (NOT QUICK COOKING)
1 LARGE EGG, BEATEN WITH 1 TBSP WATER

FOR THE TOPPING:
½ CUP ALL-PURPOSE FLOUR
½ CUP OLD-FASHIONED ROLLED OATS (NOT QUICK COOKING)
½ CUP FIRMLY PACKED DARK BROWN SUGAR
½ TSP GROUND CINNAMON
¼ TSP SALT
½ STICK (4 TBSP) UNSALTED BUTTER, MELTED

FOR THE FILLING:
2 ¾ CUPS THICK JAM OR CRANBERRY SAUCE

Makes 24 bars
Vegetarian

1 Preheat the oven to 350°F. Grease the bottom and sides of a 9 x 13-inch baking pan with butter.

2 In a food processor, whirl the flour, brown sugar, and salt to blend. Add the butter and pulse until the pieces are the size of small peas, about 30 short pulses. Add the oats, pulse a few times, then add the egg mixture in a slow, steady stream through the feed tube while pulsing. Continue pulsing until the mixture is evenly moist and crumbly, scraping the dough off the sides of the work bowl if necessary. Scatter the dough in the prepared pan and press it into a roughly even layer. Bake until lightly browned at the edges, about 20 minutes.

3 Meanwhile, make the streusel topping: Stir the flour, oats, brown sugar, cinnamon, and salt to blend in a small bowl. Add the melted butter and stir until evenly moist.

4 When the crust is toasted, remove from the oven. Carefully spread the jam in an even layer over the crust. Sprinkle the topping over the jam, and return to the oven to bake until the streusel is browned, about another 45 minutes.

5 Transfer the pan to a rack to cool completely. Cut into bars and serve.

DRUNKEN CRANBERRIES

From Sean Halligan, Urbane

This is a quick, tremendously simple winter recipe that provides multiple benefits with minimal effort. There are two final products: the rum-infused cranberries and the cranberry-infused rum. The berries are tart and tasty little flavor pellets that make a cute cocktail garnish, while the sweet-tart rum makes the finest champagne cocktail ever invented. The citrus and spices give it a generally festive scent and flavor, and the complete jar is a lovely hostess gift. The rum you choose is up to you. While this would be a bit of a waste for top-shelf stuff, don't expect the flavorings to entirely disguise the harsh burn from the budget labels.

¾ CUP SUGAR
2 CINNAMON STICKS
GRATED ZEST AND JUICE
    FROM 1 ORANGE
GRATED ZEST AND JUICE
    FROM 1 LIME

1 CUP FRESH CRANBERRIES
1½ CUPS RUM OF YOUR CHOICE,
    LIGHT OR DARK

Makes 1 quart

1 In a medium saucepan, heat the sugar and ¾ cup water over medium heat until the sugar dissolves. Add the cinnamon sticks and both citrus zests and juices. Bring to a quick boil and add the cranberries. Cook for a couple of minutes over high heat; the skins will begin cracking and making audible *pop* noises fairly quickly. Remove from the heat and cool slightly.

2 Pour the mixture into a quart-sized container with a tight-fitting lid, and top with the rum. Cool completely; then cover and refrigerate. Let sit for several days before using. Stored in the fridge, this will last for months.

Edible Tip

After the berries and rum are fully infused (up to a week), you can strain the solids from the liquids if you like. The flavored rum stores nicely at room temperature, while you can pack the cranberries into a smaller container, cover with fresh rum, and store in the fridge.

Washington's cranberry season typically falls in October. You can find Rainier Mountain Cranberries selling at the University District Farmers' Market for a few weeks each year; sign up for their market newsletter to be alerted for the specific and very short season (see Resources, page 162).

TAYBERRY HONEY SPRITZER

Tayberries deserve to be more popular than they are. Granted, their tangled mess of thorny vines is almost as bad as our invasive blackberries, but the berries are so delicious that they're worth the "berry jungle" landscaping problem. Named after Scotland's Tay River, tayberries are a cross between loganberries and raspberries and have eating qualities from both parents: the sweet hit of raspberry followed by the complex floral tartness of the best blackberries—all topped off with a gorgeous deep violet-red color. Pick up a pint at the farmers' market; eat half the berries on the way home and make a few spritzers with the remaining berries. If you aren't able to find tayberries, try this with a mix of half blackberries and half raspberries. The flavor isn't quite the same, but it's still delicious.

½ **PINT FRESH TAYBERRIES**
4 **TBSP MILD HONEY**
48 **OZ CLUB SODA OR**
   SPARKLING WINE

Makes 4 spritzers

1 Add a few ice cubes to 4 highball glasses. Divide half the berries equally among the glasses and drizzle 1 tablespoon of honey over each mound of berries. Using a long-handled spoon or narrow spatula, gently press the berries and honey together until the ice is coated with a fairly thick paste.

2 Divide the remaining berries among the glasses; then add the club soda or sparkling wine. Stir gently and serve immediately.

Edible Tip

Edible honey sampler:
- *Apple blossom:* A pale honey that's as sweet and mild as its springtime source. If you pay attention, you'll catch light fruit overtones, but they're subtle.
- *Blackberry/raspberry:* These similar varieties offer a light amber color and a pleasantly fruity flavor.
- *Buckwheat:* This dark amber honey has a distinct flavor of wholegrain buckwheat. It's fun to use in baking, but we would recommend it in ice cream only to those who think whole wheat ice cream sounds appealing.
- *Clover:* Pale gold and mildly floral, this is one of the best-selling honey varieties in the country.
- *Madrone:* Our indigenous broadleaf evergreen tree creates a unique amber honey with a peppery kick.
- *Meadowfoam:* This miraculously sweet honey has definite vanilla flavor notes. If you like cream soda, this will be your favorite honey.
- *Wildflower:* Not all honeys with this label will taste or look the same—just as wildflowers themselves vary. You can expect strong floral qualities and generally a medium-gold color.
- *Yellow starthistle:* This pale gold honey is at once light and complex, like an Irish tenor. This thistle is considered an invasive species in Washington, so this varietal's tastiness is something of a mixed blessing.

APRIUM SANGRIA

If sangria gets too sweet, you might as well drink Kool-Aid—but when it's done right, there's no more refreshing punch. Apriums come in a variety of colors and flavors, depending on which apricot and which plum were its parents. Whichever ones you choose (their season runs all summer long; Tiny's Organic offers dozens), this sangria will have floral notes, some juicy sweetness, and a hint of spicy tartness from the cherries. While sangria pairs nicely with fresh herbs and summery meals (try it with Salmon Tacos, page 90), it's at its loveliest when you're lazing around a sunny backyard with friends; the meal is optional.

¾ CUP PITTED SOUR CHERRIES
¾ CUP SUGAR
2 CUPS VODKA
8 APRIUMS OR PLUMCOTS PEELED, PITTED, AND DICED
1 (750 ML) BOTTLE SAUVIGNON BLANC

3 (12 OZ) BOTTLES DRY CUCUMBER SODA

Serves 6
Vegan
Gluten-free

1 In a small saucepan over medium heat, combine the cherries and sugar, stirring and pressing the fruit to extract the juice and dissolve the sugar. Remove from the heat as soon as all the sugar is dissolved and let cool. Combine the cherries and vodka in a small pitcher and refrigerate overnight.

2 The next day, strain out the cherries, pressing the fruit firmly to extract plenty of juice. In a large pitcher, gently blend the cherry-flavored vodka with the apriums, then slowly pour in the bottle of Sauvignon Blanc, stirring gently. Chill for at least 3 hours.

3 To serve, add a few ice cubes to a highball glass and fill the glass two-thirds of the way with sangria, using a spoon if necessary to make sure each glass has a generous serving of fruit. Top up with Dry cucumber soda and gently stir to combine.

Edible Tips

If you'd prefer a stronger herbal flavor, try the Dry lavender soda; if you'd like to accentuate the tartness of the cherries, the blood orange is a nice option. These seriously fizzy sodas add a punch of flavor without any additional sweetness.

The goal for the wine is simple: not too sweet, not too acidic. If you have a go-to white, by all means use it. Chateau Ste. Michelle's Sauvignon Blanc hits just the right balance.

DOUGLAS FIR SYRUP AND SPRITZER

From Ubon Leonard, The Herbfarm

Herbfarm proprietor Ron Zimmerman has been rummaging around in Washington's forests and waterways for several decades, making creative use of native species. Combine his knowledge and curiosity with a staff position that is unique to the Herbfarm—"nonalcoholic beverage sommelier"—and you end up with an endless list of complex beverages that changes with the seasons. For nondrinking gastronomes, there's no finer place to dine. Ubon, the talented beverage sommelier, further localized Ron's fir syrup into a spritzer made with white verjuice—a fresh grape product that the Herbfarm sources from Oregon, and we expect to see more of it from Washington, as our wine industry continues growing. If for some reason you don't have Douglas fir trees easily available, you can also use the fresh tips of noble, brand, balsam, or alpine firs. Don't be misled into thinking of air freshener: this is more like a walk in a nearby forest, lightened with the barest touch of citrus.

Edible Tip

The season for fresh Douglas fir tips varies a bit from year to year, depending on the weather, but they can be reliably found in late spring or very early summer. To be sure your foraging doesn't harm the tree, never pick tips from the tops of young trees, and never remove more than one-third of the tips from a single tree.

FOR THE DOUGLAS FIR SYRUP:
1 CUP SUGAR
2 CUPS FRESH DOUGLAS FIR TIPS (THE LAST 4–6 INCHES STRIPPED FROM THE TWIG), RINSED
¼ CUP FRESH LEMON JUICE

FOR THE DOUGLAS FIR SPRITZER:
1 CUP DOUGLAS FIR SYRUP
½ CUP WHITE VERJUICE
16 OZ (2 CUPS) CHILLED SPARKLING WATER

Makes about 2 cups syrup and 4 spritzers

Make the syrup:

1 Combine the sugar and 2 cups water in a medium saucepan. Bring to a boil over high heat. Add the fir tips, remove from the heat, and let the mixture steep for 1 hour. While it's steeping, stir the mixture once or twice. Cover and let the infusion rest for several hours or overnight.

2 Strain the syrup through a fine mesh sieve; then stir in the lemon juice. Store in a bottle with a snug-fitting lid; it will keep in the fridge for several months.

Make the spritzers:

3 Combine the syrup and verjus in a pitcher and stir gently to combine. Add the sparkling water, stir gently, and divide among 4 tall glasses. Serve immediately.

ELDERFLOWER SYRUP

From Amy Pennington

Some food you can't buy from a farm—you have to get out into the woods and work for it. In this case, "work" means picking flowers from low-hanging tree branches. It is as painless and sweet-smelling a task as you could wish for; elderberry trees are related to honeysuckles. Elderflowers blossom between the middle of May and the end of June, depending on the weather and tree location (shade and high altitude equal later blooms). We've spotted trees from Federal Way to Wenatchee. Don't strip any tree bare when you do go picking. Come September, the flowers will have converted to sweet berries, which are great for jam, syrup, and cordials. Birds and other wild critters love them, too. If you're too rushed to go hunt for a tree, you can find blossoms for sale in June at the Foraged & Found farmers' market stall.

30 ELDERFLOWER CLUSTERS
4 CUPS SUGAR
GRATED ZEST AND JUICE OF
  1 LEMON

2 TSP CITRIC ACID (AVAILABLE
  IN THE VITAMIN SECTION OF
  MOST STORES)

Makes about 4 cups

1 Place the flower clusters in a large bowl and cover with 4 cups water. Make sure the blossoms stay submerged, and let it sit out on the counter for 2 days.

2 Strain out the blossoms and discard. In a medium saucepan over medium heat, heat the blossom-infused water; then add the sugar and stir until dissolved. Remove promptly from the heat and stir in the lemon zest and juice.

3 Pour the liquid through a fine-mesh strainer lined with dampened cheesecloth, straining out any residual petals and the lemon zest. Add the citric acid, stirring to dissolve. Bottle the syrup in an airtight container and refrigerate for up to 8 weeks.

Edible Tip

Things to do with Elderflower Syrup:
• Use the syrup in place of your usual sugar when making fresh lemonade.
• Combine a couple of ounces and a dash of orange bitters with sparkling wine for a summery champagne cocktail
• Use 3 cups of the syrup and your ice cream maker to make elderflower sorbet. Serve with anise hyssop sablés (Endless Sablés, page 149).
• Substitute for St. Germain liqueur to make any elderflower-based cocktail nonalcoholic.

CHAMOMILE SYRUP

From Amy Pennington

Dainty chamomile flowers are best known as a comforting tisane—even Peter Rabbit's mother knew to calm her bunny with chamomile tea after his misadventures in Mr. McGregor's garden—but this honey-sweetened syrup also makes a fine cooler on a hot afternoon, with cucumber, seltzer, and perhaps a splash of cognac. It also serves as a delicious flavoring for a poppy-seed tea cake—just brush the syrup on after baking, while the cake is still warm. It's easy to find chamomile growing in sidewalks and retaining walls all over town, but ideally your chamomile has been picked from a spot where there's minimal contact with pollution from cars or animals. If you don't happen to have any in your garden, stop in at Tensing Momo at Pike Place Market or Dandelion Botanical in Ballard for high-quality dried chamomile flowers.

2 TBSP DRIED CHAMOMILE FLOWERS
   OR 1 TBSP FRESH CHAMOMILE
   FLOWER HEADS
2 CUPS BOILING WATER
¼ CUP HONEY

Makes about 2 cups
Vegetarian
Gluten-free

1 Put the chamomile flowers into a muslin steeping bag or a fine-mesh tea strainer. Steep in the boiling water until the liquid is stained yellow and perfumed, about 20 minutes.

2 Press any reserved liquid out from the muslin bag and discard the solids. Add the honey to the hot liquid and stir until dissolved. Store in a clean bottle in the fridge, where it will last for several weeks.

Edible Tip

Chamomile seeds are quite small and thin, so be sure to use a fine-mesh tea strainer so they don't escape and float in your syrup.

If you don't have a handy wild patch of chamomile, you can find seeds for several varieties. Typical are Spanish, English, German, and Roman chamomile, although German is the most common for culinary purposes. It's easy to grow and will reseed itself year after year (see Resources, page 162).

FARMERS' MARKETS

Seattle has four separate market management organizations. Check their websites for vendors, hours of operation, and seasonal market information.

NEIGHBORHOOD FARMERS MARKET ALLIANCE Broadway, Columbia City, Lake City, Phinney, University District, West Seattle *SeattleFarmersMarkets.org*

PIKE PLACE MARKET *PikePlaceMarket.org*

QUEEN ANNE FARMERS' MARKET *QAFMa.net*

SEATTLE MARKETS Ballard, Fremont, Georgetown, Madrona, Wallingford *FremontMarket.com*

MEAT, CHEESE, AND EGGS

APPEL FARMS This Ferndale farmstead creamery makes a slightly sweet paneer and a tasty yogurt cheese called quark, which is available in full-fat, low-fat, and nonfat varieties at numerous grocers around Puget Sound. You can find a larger selection of their cheeses and curds at occasional farmers' markets. *Appel-Farms.com*

DOG MOUNTAIN FARM Known for their duck eggs and chickens, David and Cindy Krepky also offer whole rabbits and holiday turkeys. Their farm hosts beautiful farm dinners during the summer, and Cindy developed the School of the Lost Arts, a nonprofit organization dedicated to teaching homesteader crafts to kids and adults. *DogMtnFarm.com*

FARMSTEAD MEATSMITH This Vashon Island company teaches butchering classes and sells custom slaughtering packages—butcher Brandon Sheard says that by utilizing traditional charcuterie practices, a family can eat for three years from a single pig. *FarmsteadMeatsmith.com*

GOLDEN GLEN CREAMERY Their delicious farmstead butter—lightly salted, or with seasonal flavoring ingredients—from the Skagit Valley is great for baking with or buttering your morning toast. They also make an extensive selection of cheeses, from an aged Parmesan to fromage blanc. *GoldenGlenCreamery.com*

GOTHBERG FARMS Rhonda Gothberg's fresh and aged farmstead goat cheeses are a marvel, from their creamy gouda to the Lady of La Mancha, rubbed with a beautiful red jacket of smoked paprika. In spring and summer, the chèvre and feta are outstanding. *GothbergFarms.com*

SAMISH BAY CHEESE From their award-winning Ladysmith cheese to their delectable Greek yogurt and labneh, this Skagit Valley creamery turns out top-notch dairy products. To close the loop, they also produce whey-fed pork. *SamishBayCheese.com*

SEA BREEZE FARM Combining polyculture animal grazing practices with traditional European charcuterie, their farm store and farmers' market stands offer beef, lamb, veal, pork, eggs, chickens, and raw milk. Sausages, headcheese, pâté, and chicken liver mousse are regular offerings. The farm and adjoining restaurant are on Vashon Island. *SeaBreezeFarm.net*

JONES CREEK FARMS, SEDRO-WOOLLEY

SKAGIT RIVER RANCH George and Eiko Vojkovich raise excellent grass-fed beef and pastured pork, chickens, and seasonal turkeys. Their farm store and farmers' market stands offer the best selection of sausages and unusual cuts, or you can order a family pack direct from the farm. Their eggs are a hot commodity as well. *SkagitRiverRanch.com*

STOKESBERRY SUSTAINABLE FARM Known for their eggs and chickens, this South Sound farm willingly listens to their customers— it's why they now sell whole rabbits and ducks. *StokesberrySustainableFarm.com*

SEAFOOD

CAPE CLEARE SALMON The favorite salmon supplier to several downtown restaurants, Cape Cleare boats handle their salmon individually and with care— each one is caught by hook and line, just like you would do if you went on a sportfishing trip. They're frozen as quickly as possible, resulting in firm-textured, nonmushy meat when you're ready to cook. The company ships directly from October through April—when they're not out on their boats—and the fish can be purchased at several Port Townsend locations throughout the year. *CapeCleare.com*

LUMMI ISLAND WILD To purchase the gorgeous reefnet salmon directly from Lummi Island, you need to be a member of a buying club—it's easy to start one, and some CSAs already offer the fish as an add-on purchase to their members. You can also find the fish at a few area grocers and restaurants. *LummiIslandWild.com*

MUTUAL FISH This decades-old Rainier Valley fishmonger can supply you with anything from a gorgeous Copper River King to a bag of bones for fish stock. Not all their choices are sustainable, but you'll find plenty of wonderful choices and informed fishmongers who can supply you with the answers to any fishy question you might dream up. *MutualFish.com*

SEAFOOD WATCH We urge you to start all your seafood dining experiences with a peek at the most recent Seafood Watch card for your region. These wallet cards are updated twice a year and provide the most current sustainability recommendations for numerous species. Divided into three categories ("best choice" "good choice," and "avoid"), the fish are listed in compact form with just enough information so you can ask the wait staff or fishmonger about the source. The information is also available as an app. *SeafoodWatch.org*

SEATTLE CAVIAR COMPANY Not all caviars are created equal—and sadly, some of the best-tasting varieties in the world have especially rotten sustainability records. Thanks to the dedicated sourcing of Dale and Betsy Sherrow, caviar lovers will find several gorgeous choices that earn high ratings in regard to both flavor and the overall health of the species. From ecologically farmed sturgeon (both domestic and international) to chum salmon, golden whitefish, and the delectable paddlefish, these carefully chosen caviars offer luxurious (and guilt-free) experiences. *Caviar.com*

TAYLOR SHELLFISH Home of the highest-rated oysters in the United States, the waters of Totten Inlet have combined with the dedicated efforts and refined palates at Taylor Shellfish to produce exceptional bivalves of many varieties. Whether your interests run to our tiny native Olympia oysters or to the porn star of the Pacific Ocean, the geoduck, Taylor can provide you with sustainably raised, pristine shellfish. Not all varieties are available year-round, but every season offers a good selection. Taylor is the only source for Shigoku oysters. *TaylorShellfish.com*

WILD SALMON SEAFOOD MARKET Along with a terrific array of seasonal fresh fish, the shelves of this market are stocked with a substantial selection of canned, dried, and smoked seafood from small fishing boats based in Washington and Alaska. The fresh options arrive daily and, while not all choices are sustainable, you'll find plenty of quality products and recipe cards, too. *WildSalmonSeafood.com*

PANTRY STAPLES/
ARTISANAL PRODUCTS

ALVAREZ FARMS A certified organic producer of roasted peanuts and several kinds of beans, they also raise more than 200 varieties of pepper, including the Mango Sweet, a variety unique to this Yakima Valley farm. Because their dried beans have a shorter time in storage than commercial brands, they cook much faster than you might expect. They have stands at 14 different farmers' markets.

BIG JOHN'S PFI Most famous for its fantastic cheese counter (minimum purchase is a pound per variety), PFI is also home to a vast selection of dried pasta, rice and lentils, imported syrups and canned goods, and tempting sweets. Lines are longest around major holidays, because it's known far and wide as the perfect place to stock up for a party. *BigJohnsPFISeattle.com*

BLUEBIRD GRAIN FARMS Their certified organic emmer shows up on menus all over town, but they also sell freshly milled flours made from emmer and three different kinds of wheat (they even have a pastry flour from soft white wheat), hot cereals, baking mixes, and honey from their neighbor's farm. *BluebirdGrainFarms.com*

CHEFSHOP Both a Lower Queen Anne shop and a complete online pantry store, here you can find everything from local bitters to direct-shipped fresh cherries (in season). Beans, grains, baking products, drinking chocolate, snacks, jam, and an incredible selection of vinegars and oils make this shop a Mecca for gastronomes. The shop offers occasional classes, book signings, and tasting events. *ChefShop.com*

CHUKAR CHERRIES Whether you're looking for jam or dried cherries for baking, Chukar will supply you with flavorful options. Dried cherries are available sweetened or no-sugar-added, from Bing, Rainier, and Montmorency cherry varieties. *Chukar.com*

DELAURENTI SPECIALTY FOOD & WINE From its locally sourced bitters to its wall of imported tomato products, this corner grocery in Pike Place Market offers top-notch edible items from around the world. Knowledgeable cheesemongers will take their time to steer you toward interesting choices (tastes provided), and you'll find numerous local breads and sausages in the deli. Bakers will love the upper floor, stocked with flours, chocolates, sugars, decorative items, and almond paste. *DeLaurenti.com*

EIGHTH WONDER Tended at a farmer-owned co-op of heirloom rice growers based in the Philippines, these gorgeous rices have a range of textures, flavors, and sizes. Some varieties are available on occasion at Seattle-area grocers. *HeirloomRice.com*

HOLMQUIST HAZELNUTS The DuChilly nuts grown at the Holmquist orchards are unlike any other hazelnut you may have tasted. The fat, almond-shaped nuts have a distinct raspberry sweetness and absolutely none of the more typical bitter notes present in the skins of other varieties. They're available roasted and raw, salted and unsalted, seasoned or dipped in chocolate; oil, butter, and flour are also made from the nuts. *HolmquistHazelnuts.com*

LA BUONA TAVOLA When you're in search of fresh imported black or white truffles (seasonally) or exceptional-quality truffle oils, salts, and butters (year-round), head directly to this small shop at Pike Place Market, where you can taste these products, along with beautiful balsamics and imported regional olive oils. *TruffleCafe.com*

LENTILS NATURALLY This fifth-generation lentil farm sits a few miles south of Spokane. Their French Green lentils are organically grown, and every step of the harvest and packaging process is handled by family members. *Lentilsnaturally.com*

LENTZ SPELT FARM Growers of several ancient grains in the north-central Cascades, this organic farm offers emmer, spelt, and einkorn in whole-grain, rolled-flake, and fresh-flour form, as well as expeller-pressed camelina oil. For interested farmers, camelina seed is offered as a feed supplement. *LentzSpelt.com*

OREGON TRUFFLE OIL All too often, imported brands are adulterated with synthetic ingredients, but this northwest truffle oil is made the way truffle oil should be made: by combining olive oil and truffles. The flavor of northwest white truffles is slightly different than the European, but offers a lush earthiness all its own. *Oregontruffleoil.com*

SAVOUR Crackers, cheese, fruit spreads, mustards, pepper sauce—this Ballard shop is the perfect stop before a picnic at the Locks or when you're in search of a particular hard-to-find condiment. Along with the edibles, you'll find a lovely selection of cookbooks and housewares. *SavourSpecialtyFoods.com*

SIMPLY THE BEST This small Pike Place Market stand is directly across from the famous fish throwers—so it can take a bit of effort to wade through the summer crowds. The effort pays off with locally sourced grains, flours, dried fruits, natural sweeteners, and assorted snacks. *SimplytheBest.net*

THEO CHOCOLATE Theo's fruity dark chocolate and their cacao nibs are excellent for baking; their chipotle drinking chocolate is one of the city's finest, with just the right touch of heat. The chocolate is all roasted onsite and is both organic and certified Fair Trade. *TheoChocolate.com*

UWAJIMAYA With its particular emphasis on Japanese grocery items, you'll find a fairly different selection here than at Viet Wah, although there is some degree of overlap. Look here for an excellent selection of rices, soy sauces, soy products, and fresh produce, occasionally including yuzu. *Uwajimaya.com*

VIET WAH For Southeast Asian noodles, grains, vinegars, and soy sauces—not to mention fresh-baked banh mi rolls—stop in at either of this large grocer's two South End locations. You'll also find a range of local tofu products. *VietWah.com*

WILLOWOOD FARM Between Ebey's Reserve and the Keystone ferry terminal lies a stretch of rich soil growing Whidbey's heirloom Rockwell bean, Oregon's heirloom Perigord bean, and numerous types of garlic. Both beans are pantry staples, and curious gardeners should inquire about the availability of seed beans. *WillowoodFarm.net*

WORLD SPICE MERCHANTS Tucked into the Hill Climb area adjacent to Pike Place Market, this spice shop blends ingredients for a lengthy list of Puget Sound's most renowned restaurants. You'll find plenty of tasty-smelling jars of custom curries and blends, as well as a sizable selection of individual spices and salts. *WorldSpice.com*

WILD FOOD

FORAGED & FOUND EDIBLES In addition to providing numerous restaurants with fresh and unusual wild ingredients, you can find this vendor at several Seattle-area farmers' markets during most of the year. On their table, you'll spot everything from fiddleheads to mushrooms (dried and fresh) to berries (fresh and frozen). Their website includes seasonal information for all their products. *ForagedandFoundEdibles.com*

NORTHWEST WILD FOODS Providing exceptional frozen wild berries, Wild Harvest saves you the trouble of planning your own hunts. Their berries are flash frozen the same day they're picked and are shipped on dry ice. In addition to four native berry varieties (cascade blackberry, red huckleberry, blue huckleberry, and mountain blueberries), they offer jams and honeys sourced from these species. *NWWildFoods.com*

PUGET SOUND MYCOLOGICAL SOCIETY Before going in search of your own wild mushrooms, it's important to learn from the experts. PSMS offers several levels of classes, which include informative hunting tips, mushroom lore, identification lessons, and hands-on instruction. This society can help connect you with smaller groups in your immediate area, as well as providing newsletters, events, and new friends to go foraging with. *PSMS.org*

BEVERAGE RESOURCES

BOTTLEWORKS Wallingford's palace of beer features upward of 900 varieties—you'll find cellared vintages and seasonal flavors along with full kegs and taps (they fill growlers). A small but excellent selection of meads and craft ciders rounds things off. *BottleworksBeerStore.blogspot.com*

DRY SODA Deliciously unsweet with plenty of intense flavors, these sodas can be found on cocktail menus all over town—they're just as great as mixers as they are on their own. Many regional grocers carry at least a few of the flavor choices. *DrySoda.com*

FULL THROTTLE BOTTLES Wine, beer, mead, and soda—it's a fizzy paradise in the midst of Georgetown. Owner Ericka Cowan is a cider aficionado, and the sizable cider department includes numerous choices from Northwest craft producers. *FullThrottleBottles.com*

NW CIDER ASSOCIATION Cider fiends need look no further than this regional organization for information on the latest and greatest cider varieties and tasting events. *NWCider.com*

REMEDY TEAS More like a sweet-smelling science lab than a traditional teashop, its shelves contain 150 types of organic loose tea. Whether you're looking for a specific regional black tea or a sampling of herbal blends, if it's grown organically, you're sure to find it. *RemedyTeas.com*

ROCKRIDGE ORCHARDS Wade Bennett Makes seemingly infinite beverages from his pear and apple orchards. At his farm stand on Highway 2, you'll find sweet ciders, hard ciders, fruit wines, and exceptional apple brandy—not to mention cider vinegars, mead, or the occasional eau de vie. At his farmers' market booths, you'll find everything but the distilled spirits. *RockridgeOrchards.com*

WASHINGTON WINE COMMISSION For information on the state's American Viticultural Areas (AVAs), wine tours, events, maps, vineyards, and tasting rooms, the wine commission's website is the perfect starting point. *WashingtonWine.org*

GARDENING

IRISH EYES This Ellensburg-area seed company sells to market gardeners around the country but also offers seeds in noncommercial quantities. Many interesting choices are available, including a wide range of sunflowers, cover crops, garlic, and potatoes. Not every seed offered is certified organic, but the majority of them are. *IrishEyesGardenSeeds.com*

POTATO GARDEN An excellent source for small quantities of the Ozette seed potato, a Slow Food Ark of Taste and Presidium Project. *PotatoGarden.com*

PURE POTATO/DICK BEDLINGTON FARMS For farms and market gardeners in search of large quantities of Ozette seed potatoes, this Lynden-based farm offers seed in minimum 50-pound bags. *BedlingtonFarms.com*

RAINTREE NURSERY Offers a huge selection of interesting edible plants, including fruit trees, grapevines, and berry plants of all kinds, as well as numerous heirloom varieties and unusual imports from around the world, many of which have been selected to perform well in our maritime climate. *RaintreeNursery.com*

UPRISING SEEDS This Bellingham-based organic seed website offers more than 100 vegetable and flower seed varieties, including mushroom-cultivating kits and the hard-to-find Rockwell seed beans from Whidbey Island. *UprisingOrganics.com*

ACKNOWLEDGMENTS FROM TRACEY RYDER

Edible Communities would like to thank our cofounder, Carole Topalian, for being willing to leave behind the bliss of her "semi-retired" status only to hit the road (and studio) again so this book could be filled with her beautiful and compelling images. We would also like to thank Jill Lightner for being one smart cookie, an absolute pleasure to work with, and an amazing writer, editor, recipe developer, and cook, and for her very particular and poignant dream of what a finishing school ought to be! We send big hugs and enormous thanks to Elissa Altman, our grace-under-pressure managing editor whose sense of humor and astonishing intellect can keep a team forging ahead, no matter how close the deadline looms! We also send our heartfelt thanks to the tireless recipe testers and stylists who brought these dishes to life for us in the kitchen and studio.

We also thank our agent, Lisa Ekus, for enthusiastically jumping in when we needed her most, and Alex Corcoran, publisher of *Edible Seattle*, for a lovely and important Edible magazine. And to the team Sterling Publishing, we offer our sincere gratitude for helping shepherd this series of cookbooks along, especially Carlo DeVito, Diane Abrams, Chris Thompson, Leigh Ann Ambrosi, and Blanca Oliveri.

No book is born in a vacuum, and I feel especially honored to have the pleasure of working with a team so talented and unselfish as this one is. Viva la collaborators!

—Tracey Ryder, Cofounder, Edible Communities, Inc.
Santa Barbara, California
September 2011

ACKNOWLEDGMENTS FROM JILL LIGHTNER

Edible Seattle heaps praise onto the heads of all those who contributed recipes; your talent and love for local ingredients are a pleasure to behold, and the rest of the country should be crippled with envy that they don't get to eat in your kitchens and restaurants on a regular basis. Equal credit goes to the farmers, fishermen, vintners, cheesemakers, foragers and orchardists of Washington, without whom our plates would be bland and nearly bare. You share your work with the world, but we get the best of it. A special gold star for all of you who sell at farmers markets. Your willingness to be pestered by our writers and readers make us all more informed and excited about what we eat.

Special thanks to our contributors, who make the magazine so gorgeous, smart, entertaining and delicious, and collectively are an endless font of brilliance. Jess Thomson, your palate contributes more to this book, and to the magazine, than we can possibly summarize here. Melissa Petersen, whenever we get praise for how pretty the pages are, it's meant for your ears. Angela Murray, you're the unsung heroine of the electronic side of things. To our supporters over the years—advertisers and subscribers both—we simply couldn't exist without you. Special thanks go to Chris Nishiwaki for the wine pairings in this book, and Lara Ferroni, who contributed a handful of her gorgeous photos.

Finally, a hurrah to friends and family who give us excuses to bake pie, teach us to make pickles, show us what it means to be obsessed with cheese and licorice, have ridiculous conversations with us about the possibilities of cooking food in the dishwasher, treat us to incredible meals, and stuff yourselves at our table. Food is a lot more fun when it's shared with those we love.

—Jill Lightner, *Edible Seattle*

INDEX